BEACHED

BEACHED

Get back in the swim
when receding tides
leave you high and dry

L. R. BEERMAN

Team LRB Press
Aurora, Colorado

Beached: Get back in the swim when receding tides leave you high and dry
by L.R. Beerman

Copyright © 2011 L. R. Beerman / Lizabeth R. Beerman

This is a work of fiction. Names, characters, places, and incidents either are the product of the author's imagination or are used fictitiously, and any resemblance to actual persons, living or dead, events, or locales is entirely coincidental.

All rights reserved. No part of this publication may be reproduced, distributed, or transmitted in any form or by any means, including photocopying, recording, or other electronic or mechanical methods, without the prior written permission of the publisher, except in the case of brief quotations embodied in critical reviews and certain other noncommercial uses permitted by copyright law. For permission requests, write to the following:

Team LRB Press
23786 E. Grand Place
Aurora, Colorado 80016
USA

lrbeerman@beachedstory.com
www.beachedstory.com

Editing by Karen Reddick, The Red Pen Editor
Cover and interior design by Nick Zelinger, NZ Graphics

Beached is available at Amazon.com and BarnesandNoble.com

Ordering Information:
Quantity sales. Special discounts are available on quantity purchases by corporations, associations, and others.

Orders by U.S. trade bookstores and wholesalers.
Contact Liz Beerman at lrbeerman@beachedstory.com

ISBN: 978-0-9826296-1-1

Library of Congress Control Number: 2011925675

Self-help / personal growth
Self-help / motivational & inspirational

First Edition

Printed in the United States of America

To Jules who never fails to really see me.

Contents

Acknowledgments.................................. ix

Introduction..................................... xi

One: *She scooped up handful of warm sand*............ 1

Two: *Seagulls played tug-of-war on the sand*.......... 5

Three: *"Ahoy, there!"* 13

Four: *Sparks were spiraling in wild flight* 23

Five: *Pearl pink clouds crept up the horizon* 31

Six: *Heads bobbed with lively conversation*.......... 41

Seven: *Going from tide pool to tide pool* 45

Eight: *Today belonged to the percussions*............ 53

Nine: *Bright sun made the shells sparkle*............ 63

Ten: *Whitecaps dotted the horizon*................. 67

Eleven: *Cold, wet, squishy sand oozed up*........... 71

Twelve: *Screaming at the top of his lungs*........... 75

Thirteen: *She missed the comfortable rhythm*........ 81

Fourteen: *Too much of a summons to ignore* 85

Fifteen: *Dusk quietly descended in a velvet curtain* ... 93

Sixteen: *Ned gave up his morning run on the beach*... 97

Seventeen: *Three piercing blasts grabbed their attention*....... 103

Eighteen: *The big blue ship rocked gently* 107

Mack... 113

Now What? 117
About Liz Beerman. 121
About Susann Leasure 122
About Ken Ouellette. 122

Acknowledgments

Participating in the raising of children or teaming in a corporate acquisition task force proved somewhat less painful than the unpredictable bumps, stalls, twists, and turns in the creation, crafting, and delivery of this book. As the writing process spanned years, the political, economic, technology and social landscape evolved dramatically. That carefully constructed strategy from which I had been taking my clues, aged before my eyes and my next steps were inevitably impacted. The drummers' drums changed and as an author I had to learn to dance to several new, different, and sometimes uncomfortable beats. I am grateful to those who not only danced with me but offered encouragement and support when it was in short supply in my own stockpile. While I would prefer to shout their praises in the town square of old, I am relegated to not only this page, but to the ever-changing Internet social mediums through which I will call out my gratitude as well. These wonderful and talented people deserve gratitude, recognition and praise and I enthusiastically share that here.

Amanda Malone and I started the storytelling process over hot coffee and frustrated personal examples of being beached. Her ability to offer input and feedback on the messages found in this story, as well as hold me to those initial and elusive writing timelines was crucial to gaining traction. Karen Reddick opened her cache of experience and with great generosity shared, guided, and polished the edited manuscript, refusing to give in until we both were satisfied with the magic of *Beached*. Nick Zelinger listened carefully, considering and translating my initial vision. Then with authenticity and a gentle touch, he took the artists' gifts and fashioned them into this imaginative layout and spectacular cover. Susanne Leasure held the heart of the beach in her initial photograph. Her subsequent transformation of that photograph into this spectacular painting and then generous sharing for *Beached* was a gift beyond imagining. Ken Ouellette suspended light, time, and beauty through the lens of his camera and then took us with him to that singular breathless moment. Cade, Craig, Jennifer, Julie, Mike, Sally, and Vince–*thank you* is so inadequate. I entrusted you with the most vulnerable part of my creativity. Your respect and thoughtful feedback is visible throughout.

With gratitude,

Liz

Introduction

You lose a critical customer or worry that the next revenue project might not close. Perhaps you face a layoff, reduction in work force, or being fired. Maybe your love life ends or an unexpected illness or accident leaves you confined. Business and personal challenges confront us daily, leaving us angry, frustrated and dazed as we look for answers and direction. These trying situations make us struggle against the tide and the results leave us feeling high and dry … Beached!

By exchanging life on land for a corresponding existence on the water, the activities here; whether enterprise, manufacturing, education, research, medical, hospitality, service, or entertainment, take place on water-going vessels. Enormous industrial ships with billion-dollar payloads, luxurious cruise ships, submarines, trawlers, tankers, sailboats, motorboats and even self-propelled rafts darting in seemingly random patterns provide a multitude of services and jobs.

Water is the foundation of life. It runs through our bodies, moves us from place to place, houses substantial food sources, delivers energy, and provides multiple opportunities for our entertainment. Civilizations have consistently formed near bodies of water and fortunes are made by those who use water to their personal and business advantage.

This book is a parable about life in and on the water and six characters who find themselves unexpectedly beached. Landing here as a result of departmental reorganization, layoff, merger, death of a spouse, natural disaster, and medical diagnosis, these hardworking and dedicated people try deliberately not to "take it personally." They are simply eager to get their lives moving forward, back on the water.

Through unexpected messages and the guidance of a mysterious lighthouse keeper, each comes to grips with their current situation and faces the challenge of getting back on the water with a new sense of definition, determination, and the drive to make it happen.

Beached utilizes the stinging realities that smack us when we are down, to uncover the simple truths that inspire us to do better than just "put one foot in front of the other." Empowered with a clearer vision of the horizon, *Beached* illustrates how focusing on the present moment, coupled with commitment and support, creates an opportunity for choices that can be embraced and implemented for a lifetime.

One

She scooped up a handful of warm sand and let it slip through her fingers. Her other hand still clenched the memo that came across her desk last month, *"At the beginning of next quarter, the entire company, across all departments, will need to implement a reduction in force of 35 percent of current personnel."*

She sat motionless, remembering her reaction and thoughts about having to let some of her team go—never seeing her own layoff coming. Like a movie, she remembered sitting comfortably in her boss' office, chatting about the weather, the economy, and sports teams, until the words, "I have some bad news," tossed her like whitecaps on winter seas. She was furious. Blinding anger took control as she gripped the chair's arms, rose up, turned on her heels and deliberately walked out, slamming the door behind her.

Shifting her left foot on top of the sand, raising both hands above her head, she released the paper into the nearest gust of wind. *Now what?* she thought.

The sun wound its way across the sky and the wind gently rustled the palms overhead. She tilted her head toward the sun letting its warmth take her back to other days, on other beaches. Under different circumstances she would have considered it a perfect morning. As if in a mirage she saw friends and family eating, drinking, and playing. She heard their laughter. She saw the stuff of which ideal vacations are made.

Vacations. Holidays. Time away from the daily grind of work and its responsibilities. Lazy days that invited rest for mind and body. She longed for those long walks, sculptured sand castles, and treasures in the surf. She recalled those "what if" conversations laying out potential adventures allowing her to be anyone, to live anywhere, to have anything desired by the heart. The shrill squawk from a nearby seagull snapped her back to this beach.

Three days ago she had been out there, on the water, on what she believed, was her ship of dreams—a corporate path to her future. She looked out now and saw the industrial steamers with billion-dollar payloads crisscrossing the watery expanse alongside luxurious cruise ships, sluggish barges, and stately, determined military vessels. Services transports defined the routes between them all, delivering required lifelines of energy, communication, and fuel, both for the ships and their personnel.

She surveyed this world with all that work taking place on, in, or under the water. She thought how businesses flourish on the face of the sea, rivers, and lakes, as they have for ages. *It is out there that fortunes are made and dreams come true,* she thought. There are as many sizes of floatable devices as there are visions crafted by pilots and their crews. She considered the accepted theory that until recently, the size of the vision matched the size of the vessel: ships, submersibles, boats, barges, tugs, canoes, kayaks, rafts and everything in between. Now, it seemed the possibility of realizing great revenue could happen from even the most unlikely places. The water is the playing field. The beach isn't even in the game, *and now I'm stuck on the sidelines!*

Gazing over the water, she remembered the first day she boarded TNL, Inc. Her shiny engraved nameplate was on the cubicle wall adjacent to the entrance of her new world. Kate Windsor, Software Team. Over the next seven years she kept her head down and her deliverables on time. She learned the political and business processes that helped her successfully and profitably work her way up the ladder. Now, as team supervisor amid daunting economic challenges, extreme quotas and shrinking budgets imposed by upper management, she and her staff exceeded all expectations. Reorganize the department and layoff key management positions like hers? How could she have been so clueless?

With her heart in her throat, and holding fear at bay, again she asked herself, *now what?* She was on the sand and the action was on the ships. She needed a way to get back on the water, back in the game.

Start with a plan. Define your resources. Identify and prepare for the liabilities. Good ideas. They had always worked for her in the past. She decided to strike out and find out exactly what she was dealing with here. Being beached was one thing, doing nothing was not an option.

She stood up, adjusted her sunglasses, left her high heels and suit jacket on a piece of driftwood, and started walking down the beach.

Two

The mid-afternoon sun danced on the back of each wave as it took its time rolling up the sand bluff. Seagulls and sandpipers ran back and forth joining the water's ritual with playful squawks and squeals. She watched as two seagulls played tug-of-war on the sand with what looked like a knotted ball of pale seaweed. Their antics were comical as they ran first one way and then another, all the while tugging and twisting.

Curious, Kate walked a bit closer and realized it wasn't seaweed at all. It was a brown paper bag that looked like someone's forgotten lunch. Judging from the size and sagging bottom, it seemed there would be plenty for both these scavengers. The tugging went on until, unexpectedly, one of them grabbed the bag and struggled to fly. Sensing the vulnerability caused by the added weight, the other swooped wide. Feathers flew as their competition for the gourmet prize became more furious.

"Silly birds," Kate said with a smile. "Just cooperate, would you? There's plenty there for you, and most of your friends."

Kate couldn't contain her laughter as the bag tore open and a shower of sandwich, napkin, cookies and fruit spilled down as quickly as the surprised seagulls flew up. Their awkward flight had taken them over the crashing waves. The next wave broke in a spray of whitewater just as their treasures hit and promptly sank. Continuing to smile, she watched both birds circle above the wreckage desperately looking for prized remains.

If only they had realized the rewards available in leveraging their individual strengths. Instead, there they were, hungry and perched on the beach, gazing out at the water, and the spoiled plan. Kate's thoughts turned back to her job. She knew all about teamwork. Her team never sat wondering what to do next. They were consistently recognized for exceeding goals, delivering projects before they were due, and then offering to help other departments move along. Clear on this goal to get back in the water, she decided she would most likely need the help of others to accomplish it. She decided to set out and find them.

Having perfected the art of leveraging and negotiating through her business dealings, she prided herself in her ability to identify and maximize the talents of others. Walking boldly down the beach, she worked to convince herself that this was the same thing. Didn't everyone here want to get back to the water? Surely she could be a catalyzing force and make a difference for more than just her own goal.

Remnants of the brown lunch package washed up on the sand. Walking closer she thought she saw writing on the bag. The name of a deli perhaps; she couldn't quite make it out, yet the writing appeared to sparkle. Her interest piqued. Bending down to get a better look she blinked as the sparkles wiggled on the paper and bright purple words appeared:

CONNECT DELIBERATELY

She stepped back cautiously and quickly looked around to see if anyone else was nearby. Spotting a rather intriguing looking gentleman just ahead she called out, "Hello, there."

With pant legs rolled up, a baseball cap on backwards and a smooth, driftwood walking stick in hand, he strolled down the beach, poking at seaweed. He turned, smiled, and responded, "Hello, yourself."

Did you see that bag . . . that message?" she exclaimed, a bit too loudly pointing behind her. "It's right there with the sparkling writing. Can you see it?" She was almost breathless as she hurried to catch up with him.

"Slow down, my dear," he said brushing his calloused, sandy hand on the side of his pants. "You seem surprised. Everyone gets messages every day. Some by mail, some by phone, some shouted down the hall, and even some by more primitive methods. Don't you receive messages, in some form or another every day?"

"Well, yes, I suppose," she offered, "but they don't usually appear out of nowhere." Turning back to double check her discovery, she found the words had disappeared and the soggy brown bag lay in a wet heap on the sand.

"Let's walk for a bit," he offered.

Kate felt queasy and unnerved. She recognized herself as a certifiable control freak with generally enough attention to detail for herself and her entire team. Not a big fan of surprises or unexpected events, the last few moments had left her feeling uncharacteristically out of control. *What do I have to do to move forward and get on with my real life?*

Mack had already moved along and without looking back at her said, "But that's exactly what you are doing, my friend . . . you're getting on with your life."

"Huh? How did you . . ." She fell in step behind him and hurried to shorten the gap between them. Deciding not to pursue the obvious mind-reading trick right now she changed the subject, "I'd really like to know more about the beach. It's beautiful here and under other circumstances would be a marvelous place to hang out." Kate smiled as she realized the silliness of standing on a beach in work clothes. She looked around to see what others were wearing and was reminded of her objective to find others and put together a team. But no one was in sight. *Curious*, she thought. As inappropriate as her outfit was to the environment, she realized how uncomfortable she felt on land and longed to be back at work on the water.

"What do you expect from the beach, Kate?"

"Excuse me?" she asked and then caught her breath with the thought that she didn't remember telling him her name. A wisp of wind brushed across her cheek and she turned her face toward the afternoon sun. Letting out a sigh and with an unfamiliar sense of resignation she continued, "Well, first, you don't find beaches like this every day. How many places can make you feel simultaneously safe and eager and at the same time unsure and anxious? I really haven't got a clue what to expect. I just know that I don't generally do well with ambiguity."

"How so?" he asked.

Slowing her pace as her eyes darted across the horizon she pulled everything she knew about the beach from her memory. Building a useable framework of knowledge, she shared with him her perception of the beach and consequences of being beached. Piecing stories of others who had been beached at various times and in various circumstances through her relationships, she related the oddity that no two stories were ever even remotely similar. Anyone with a beach story appeared to have had a singularly unique experience, as if they had all been on completely different beaches. And yet, something happens here that had equipped them to move forward. She searched futilely for a foundation of experience on which to stand.

She went on, "I can't imagine what I can reasonably expect from this beach other than soft breezes, gentle waves, perfect temperatures and soft white sand. I love it, but I can't be here for long. There must be more here that I can work with to get back on the water. I'm not looking for buried treasure, just some decent tools and insights that will point me to the resources that can help me get back to work." She wondered if he might be the perfect start to help her leverage her position.

He stopped and faced her. For the first time she noticed the depth in his crystal blue eyes and found it surprisingly effortless to match his gaze. He spoke softly, "Just be sure to enjoy those things that have been given to you here. Use the beach." He paused, cradled his walking stick in the crook of his other arm and went on, "Each of the elements that touches you has a deliberate purpose for you, Kate, and for your time here."

I wonder what that means, she thought. Acknowledging without reservation the importance of his message, even though she wasn't sure it made sense to her right now, she let the words circle aimlessly in her head. Wiggling her feet into the sand she watched a pelican make a spectacularly ungraceful landing on the water.

"When are you planning to get back in the water?" she asked him as he righted an upside down starfish and moved it back into a nearby tide pool.

"Oh my," he chuckled. "I'm not beached. This is my life. I live here. I care for the light and the lighthouse."

This is all coming too fast, she thought recapturing the queasy feeling. Not only was she still stunned by the message on the bag, but now she was captivated by the presence of the resident light keeper as well.

"Really?" he asked. "I was impressed by how steady you appeared."

"Okay, let's just stop a moment and regroup," she pleaded. "I'm overwhelmed. I need to get back in the water immediately. I have a message that I don't know what to do with, I'm totally unsure as to what to do next, I need some help to start a plan, and how do you do that mind reading trick?"

Kate grew up knowing that to be a contributing member of society; prosperous, accomplished, and defined, you needed to have a job. Somehow, right now, beached and left only to watch everyone else on the water at their jobs, she was beginning to feel useless and afraid. Maybe she was truly becoming invisible to the business world.

Without missing a beat he said, "Then let's start on more solid ground. I'm Mack."

Looking more closely at him, she recognized the weatherworn face of a long-time beach resident. The days in the wind and salt spray from the waves had written stories on his face and hands. "Did you retire here?" she asked.

"Retire? Heavens no, I'm still working, my dear," he replied. His soft eyes focused directly on her and he brightened in a smile. Nodding toward the distant lighthouse he went on, "If that light isn't cared for, if the foghorn isn't always ready, who knows how many boats and ships would crash onto those rocks? Who knows how many desperate swimmers would not be able to find their way to the beach? I try to make sure that regardless of the way the wind blows, or tries to push around those folks out on the water, there is always a point of stability they can count on."

Beached

How I wish I had seen the light before landing on the beach, she thought. Pieces of thought like jigsaw puzzles were swirling all around her. She found herself wishing for a "time out" with a tall flavored latte and a quiet place to reflect on it all.

"I can't help you with the coffee, but we can talk about landing here on the beach and your message, if you like." Without moving her head, she let out an extra-long sigh and rolled her eyes. He was doing it again.

"Okay," she said. "Tell me why I saw a message on that bag and why the message disappeared."

"Because you needed to see that message, at that moment," he replied. "This beach is just a place. It can mean, and be, whatever you want. While you arrived with your own ideas about being beached, it will be up to you to be open to the messages and support that are here for you. What you believe is more important than what you see and will impact the path you choose. Take the time to acknowledge and share everything the beach presents. Believe in more than just what you see, hear, smell, think, and feel. I'm sure you know by now that the beach, while beautiful, is not your destination. This is a stage and an opportunity for you to practice your next steps. How you use it, what you learn, how far you go, how accomplished you become is completely up to you. There is no one waiting to give you a star at the end of this project."

Kate laughed, subconsciously sitting up straight like she did in first grade, hoping for that precious gold star.

"This time it's all up to you . . . it's all *for* you, and you're the only critic who matters." With that he winked, turned the cap so the bill would shade his eyes and walked away. "Best of everything," he said. "And I mean it."

A soft gray fog of exhaustion blanketed Kate and she plopped down on the sand. Pulling her knees into her chest and wrapping her arms around them she let the concept of being beached settle in. She had two choices in front of her—worry about tomorrow or watch the seagulls gliding overhead carried by the unseen wind. She chose the seagulls but couldn't help wondering where those winds would send her next?

Three

"Ahoy, there!"

The call pulled her gaze to the right. She shaded her eyes and answered, "Hello."

"Never thought you'd end up here, huh?" he asked.

"No, I didn't," she replied. She wasn't quite ready for this intrusion into her daydream moment; however, she realized the importance of Mack's direction; to use the message and gifts of the beach. With that in mind, she decided to *connect deliberately* with this new acquaintance.

"Is this your first time?" he continued.

"Since leaving college, yes."

He sauntered toward her and she couldn't help noticing how out of place he seemed against Mack's casual attire. His pin-striped slacks ended at his shoeless winter-white feet. His jacket had been abandoned and his chest was partially visible from the top of his unbuttoned dress shirt. His necktie knotted around his upper arm reminded her of group identifiers in games like team flag football. Like a slingshot, her thoughts bounced back to her own team at work.

His pockets swelled with collected shells and the rolled cuffs of his pant legs captured bits of sand deposited by the lapping waves. "I'm Ned Buckingham." He bent down and extended his right hand.

She stood and took his hand, "Kate Windsor. You seem mighty chipper for someone who's beached. How long have you been here?"

"Obviously not long enough," he laughed. He reached in his shirt pocket and pulled out a newspaper clipping. Kate read the highlighted sentence: *The board of directors confirmed that the company filed bankruptcy and will be liquidating over the next ninety days.*

Without hesitation he went on, "However, time here is an interesting commodity. Sometimes it feels like days last forever and you haven't made any progress toward getting back on a ship. And then something unexpected happens and in minutes everything you have been doing, or collecting, or challenging will come together in a crystal clear vision. Your next steps are obvious and off you go."

"Sounds like you've been beached before," she said.

"Several times, in fact. Every time, however, has been a completely different experience. Might seem strange, I admit, but there's more here than meets the eye."

Have you figured out how to get back in the water this time?" she asked hopefully.

Ned laughed. "Well, I'm no expert on being beached but if you'll join me at the water cooler I'll share what I know." *Water cooler? On the beach?*

Ned led her away from the surf toward a nearby cliff. Here brown rocky earth met the sand at a rough and foreboding rock wall. Dotted in the crags and crevices, Kate marveled at the brilliant wildflowers taking in the rich fragrance and splatter of welcome warm color. She saw it as a real life rendition of the framed water color she loved in her parents' living room. However, she realized that nothing on this terrain looked tamed by civilization and certainly not a likely place for a traditional water cooler.

"Pull up a rock and sit," he invited her. There, surprisingly, and as promised, a fountain from a hidden spring bubbled out of the rocks creating an inviting crystal stream down to the ocean. Kate watched him reach for several large shells perched on adjoining rocks. Choosing one he stepped close to the source, filled it and carefully handed it to her. She took a sip amused at how easily this shell doubled as a drinking cup and how wonderful the water tasted. He filled another and lowered himself carefully onto a nearby rock.

"I've been here a short while this time," he began. "I was on a startup ship that had lots of funding and a darn good product." He paused. Relaxing into the start of his story, Kate eased into the comfort of finding someone else who was beached.

"I started my career several years ago on one of those megaships as part of a global fleet. The media confirmed we were headed for great recognition and the financial rewards that come with exceeding market expectations. I held a variety of positions, but over time I didn't feel like my talents and deliverables mattered as much as they once did. The hop from one ship to the other, with a bigger title and promises of new challenges, was an easy choice.

"Unfortunately, as a startup, we were spending way too much time focused on the inner workings of the ship's engine and forgot to pay as much attention to the wind's direction and speed. The ship crashed on the rocks, about a mile up the beach, and we were all thrown out."

He pointed in the direction away from the lighthouse, around the bend of the shore, out of sight. "Being with a startup company, I figured something like this might happen and I set aside provisions in case I ended up beached."

"Where are the others who landed here with you?" Kate asked.

"Oh, I suspect you'll meet some of them along the way," he smiled. "Some of them paid the fare and boarded one of those expensive ferries that take you from ship to ship in search of available openings. Others are wandering the beach, and a couple of them are inventorying pieces salvaged from the shattered boat."

Continuing on, he said, "I've bumped into all sorts of people who share the sand and surf with us. There are those who just got here and those who have been here awhile. Everyone has his own story."

Sipping her water Kate asked, "What have you learned or discovered while you've been here?"

"The beach is lovely, but it's not easy to get a good meal," he offered facetiously. "The rock wall provides some shelter from the wind, but there aren't many resources available to build a structure—temporary or otherwise. Obviously there are no laptops, no PDAs, or other electronic devices to distract you, although there are phones and Internet access over by the lighthouse. When you meet someone, the conversation always winds its way to the subject of getting off the beach, back on the water; back to a job, or relationship, or neighborhood, or life.

"There's lots of time to think and look out on the water. For those of us used to days filled with long to-do lists, ringing phones, email, voicemail, texts, meetings, reports, conference calls, and production reports, it isn't always easy.

This forced time to reflect is a break—welcome or not. It's necessary as a preparation for the next part of your life, and if you let it, it feels surprisingly right. That, however, is harder than it sounds."

They turned their attention to the breaking waves and spent the next few moments in quiet thought. Kate took advantage of the silence and allowed herself to wonder what might lie ahead. Her unfocused gaze followed a passing sailboat until it slipped out of sight but then stopped abruptly as she caught sight of someone marching quickly toward them.

"Looks like he's in a big hurry," she said.

Ned nodded as they stood.

"Is this where the drinking water is?" The man asked pushing his way past them to the fountain.

"Hi . . ." Ned began, extending his hand.

Ignoring the greeting, the man reached for an available shell knocking several others to the sand. "Why are we here?" The man grumbled mostly to himself. "What did I do wrong to end up here? You would think with everything I did to prepare for every possible eventuality, the hours I spent away from my family, the preparations that I took for protecting those I loved, that I would have been exempt from that devastating hurricane. Who's in charge here, anyway? I need something better for me and my family than this . . . this . . . beach!"

He started to stomp away and turned back. "Do either of you have any idea what I have to do to find someone with some answers?" Before either of them could respond, he kicked at the sand and stormed off.

"Wow! I sure hope he finds what he is looking for," Kate said. She continued to watch him get smaller and smaller as the distance between them grew. It was a long minute or two before she turned her attention back to Ned who now seemed quietly introspective.

"So how do you plan to get back in the water?" she asked.

"I'm not sure this time," Ned responded. "I really thought I was going to be more ready for the beach, but now I'm not so sure." His voice dropped. Kate couldn't help but shift her gaze to the face of the rocky cliff with its variegated shower of wildflower color. Each little outcropping of leaves and dainty flowers danced easily in response to intermittent sea breezes. *Wish I could be that free*, she considered.

Without looking directly at Kate, he continued, "There are more unknowns this time than I experienced before and it's taking longer than I anticipated mapping out a workable plan. I'm growing frustrated as each unproductive day rolls by. I miss my computer, my calendar, and my organizational tools. Scheduled time, to-do lists and spreadsheets were my daily compasses. I forgot what it was like to have to rely solely on my own ideas. The clock inside my head is ticking loudly, and it seems the faster I run and the harder I work on my strategy to get back in the water, the farther away any viable opportunity moves from my grasp. I'm no closer to getting off the beach today than I was a week ago."

Hearing this was not encouraging. Kate had always been the one with the answers on her team, or at the very least, suggestions for moving a project forward. She wished there were more she could offer, but her lack of experience at being beached left her with no advice. Recognizing there wasn't anything more she could say or do to make him feel better, Kate decided to leave him to his thoughts, "I think I'll walk a bit and get a lay of the land. Thank you for the water."

"See you later," he responded flatly.

Standing, she surveyed her options and decided on a path that would take her around the cliff. The intrigue of what was on the other side was irresistible. Stepping carefully between tide pools, she was awed by powerful evidence of the pounding surf against the granite and sandstone rocks. Water that was currently calm and unthreatening could do some amazing work when the tides were right. Repetitive caves, arches, and tunnels had been carved from previously impenetrable stone.

Emerging on the other side, smooth sand bays punctuated by a string of formidable cliffs continued on as far as she could see. A pod of seals basked in the late day sun. Throaty croaking and barking at her arrival appeared to signal it was time to return to the sea.

Beyond the indented seal beds and adjoining braids of tangled seaweed, Kate noticed an unusual outcropping of rocks. She walked over and saw what appeared to be a well-tended rock-rimmed fire pit. As the sun's waning path signaled day's end, she could envision the bright orange sparks dancing on a neatly piled mound of driftwood.

Memories of sticky s'mores made her lick her lips and she reveled in that long forgotten childhood memory. How simple those days had been; free from adult responsibility, free to dream, free to create, and free to make friends. What pieces of that simplicity and freedom remained now in her adult world? She marveled at how loyal and uncomplicated those friendships had been, sealed with mud and watermelon seeds. She could hear the whispered pacts of lifelong commitment—or at least until the summer ended.

A lone seagull sat a few yards away, staring at the water with an intensity that bewildered Kate. "Where are your buddies?" she asked, not expecting a response. The seagull stood perfectly still, completely ignoring this stranger on his beach.

The first faint string of whining squeals floated on the air. She recognized an approaching flock of seagulls and looked at her beach companion to see if there would be a reaction. Seven or eight seagulls flew low across the sand, and the lone seagull stayed put. Another six or seven in the distance but not until the third group appeared, did her companion spread his wings and rise to meet them.

"Why them?" she questioned. "Why did you choose to join that particular group?" Kate thought back to the message written on the lunch bag. *Connect deliberately.* She got it! She believed she now knew what the message meant. At least it held potential for a plan and the promise of forward motion.

Turning back, she noticed a cutout between this beach and the one she shared with Ned. Without hesitation, she ducked into the tunnel and emerged on the other side greeted by the sweet gurgling of the water cooler. The water from the spring bubbled softly down the rocks and merged seamlessly with the afternoon waves. She spied Ned lying on the beach, hands under his head, eyes closed.

Softly she said, "Hey Ned, I have an idea." Opening his eyes, Ned brought his hand around for shade. "You said there were others from your company here. Rather than just sit and wait to run into them, I'd like to see if we can *connect deliberately* and brainstorm ideas for a plan that could help us all get back in the water.

Ned sat up while nodding his head. "Great idea. I'd be willing to help gather as many others we can find. Where would you like to meet?"

"I found a perfect place to build a fire not far from here," Kate bent down and pointed through the tunnel.

"I know the place," he said. "You're right, there's strength in numbers. I'm sure everyone from our ship has an idea or two, especially those who have been here before. I think I know where some of them might be. I'll head off, extend the invitation, and meet you at the fire ring at nightfall," he said.

Kate smiled, "I'll begin scavenging for wood to burn."

Ned set off almost jogging down the beach. Chuckling, Kate started on her quest for firewood. Her mind raced and she felt comfortable on the more familiar turf of potential project management. She was energized at the prospect of meeting more beached colleagues. She knew she didn't have all the answers, and not even a complete understanding of what the message meant; but, one thing she was sure of, even in her reluctance to admit it to herself, this path felt right.

Kate picked up small twigs and dried grass to get the fire started, large branches to build the heat, and hefty logs to keep it going. Depositing her stash in three piles near the fire pit she stayed on the hunt until she considered the cache substantial enough to support a couple of hours of fire. Her hands felt gritty and she decided to walk to the water to wash them off while she dipped her toes in at the water's edge.

Rolling her pant legs up, she let her mind wander back to the message on the bag. *What would connecting deliberately look like?* Her collection of names, phone numbers, mailing and email addresses was lengthy: personal database, office database, church and philanthropic organizations, mobile phone list, and more than three social networks kept growing by the day. How her dad would have laughed at the systems that now replaced his critical Rolodex files from years ago. The standard black metal box sat prominently on his oversized desk—the lifeline of his business and a coveted treasure handed down from office manager to office manager. Would he have thought it absurd that her groups grew with names of people she didn't even know?

Colleagues and peers would announce in casual conversation the number of "friends" they had in different social networks. She found herself comparing, to see how she stacked up. Who had the most connections? Was this a competition? She surprised herself with the thought. I don't think I've ever actually removed a single name. And so the numbers grew, day by day, week by week. Faced with the imposing task of keeping up with it all, dashing off electronic messages, emails, voicemails and reaching out online to stay connected, stole hours from her day, and exhausted her. Was this only a frantic exercise to be sure she was not forgotten? That she mattered in someone else's world?

She wished she had those old Rolodex cards with handwritten notes reflecting true personal connections; precious, hand-forged relationships spanning years.

She mentally began reviewing her electronic contact files. With whom would she start building those dedicated and invested relationships? Where were those valued connections from which she would start reaching out? Her first step would have to be to *connect deliberately* and then nurture each relationship. While this could certainly be done electronically, it could never be done automatically. It had to be genuine, thoughtful, and deliberate.

She looked up as the seagulls continued their winged dance in the afternoon breezes. Lazy circles replaced the earlier, frenzied, lunch sack attacks. Kate felt herself pulled into the calmness of their quiet flight, wishing she too could fly above it all. Thirst hit the back of her throat and she knew she had time to head back to the water cooler before the evening group arrived. She wondered if the seagulls watched her as she walked away.

Four

Sparks were spiraling in wild flight as Kate returned to the fire ring. Ned had built the fire and new faces, illuminated by the glow, talked easily with each other. A few more walked up and moved into the ring without the need for an invitation. Kate overheard, "Isn't this a great idea?" and another voice added, "Why didn't we think about this before?" *What an interesting mix*, Kate observed. The oldest looked to be past sixty and the youngest, right out of school. Eager to join in the conversations, she wanted to learn more about each face, each story.

She immediately recognized the man walking toward her and wondered if he was still angry. "Good evening," she said tentatively.

"I'm sorry if I was rude earlier," he started. "This is just so unfair. I had a beautiful home, yard, and community before we were all hit by the hurricane. I feel so helpless. I did everything I could to protect my home and my family. While I know that first and foremost I am grateful we are all alive, I don't know what to do next. There just are no user's manuals for sorting out your life after something like this."

Kate smiled as she thought of the words her mother used years ago, *Exactly where does it say on your birth certificate that life is fair?*

"I don't know if you remember," she began, "my name is Kate."

"I'm Val Parker." He turned toward the ring and proceeded to move a large rock a few inches to the left, and another one a bit forward, so that the circle was as round as possible. He stood back to survey the scene and, deciding it was good enough, took a seat and invited Kate to join him. Kate was amused with his attention to detail. Brushing the sand off the makeshift seat, she sat down.

Darkness settled in, but the moon rising from behind the rock wall cast a golden sliver of light. The faint outline on the sand grew larger and brighter moment by moment until the entire shore dramatically beamed capturing the iridescence in the wet sand. Waves broke rhythmically sending a final soft swish on the shore before retreating.

Conversations grew louder and more animated as people introduced themselves to each other. Stories bantered back and forth with gestures and facial expressions demonstrating a full range of sentiments. Kate turned to Val and asked him to tell her more about the disaster. While she had read about it in the paper, she knew his firsthand account was much more powerful—and emotional. He looked down at his feet and began to move them slowly in the sand.

"Mother Nature has a strange way of sharing her planet with us," he started. "I guess I should have seen it coming. We were warned by the old timers that something like this could happen—someday. When you are young and just starting out you don't listen. You feel invincible and bigger than any potentialities of weather." A loud snap from the fire sent a cinder flying across the ring landing at Val's feet.

Momentarily distracted, he watched it glow before continuing, "There was no way to prepare for the moment we returned to the address that had once been our home. My son's bicycle sat completely unharmed—six feet up in the broken branches of a neighbor's tree. Pieces of everyone's lives; furniture, vehicles, photo albums, kitchen utensils, were mixed together and scattered from one end of our block to the other. Years of acquired treasures and memories had been whirled together in a giant mixer and poured out without regard to owner or location." His voice broke and he gulped hard before going on, "But the worst, I guess, is the feeling of helplessness. My wife and I are a great team. We have always patched the wrongs and mended the broken wings for our children. This time we just couldn't make it right. No amount of words from our motivational or philosophical archives could explain this away. Now we are all in a perilous and rocky mix of anger, frustration, and despair." He sighed heavily and with rounded shoulders and visible resignation picked up the cooled bit of charcoal at his feet, and tossed it into the fire, "I guess being angry doesn't do much good."

"Where do you go when home isn't home anymore?" Kate whispered. "This uncertainty must be scary when so many others depend on you."

"I know I have to begin rebuilding and I just want to get back home. I can do this. I'm good at mapping out a strategy for us. It's just tough to see a clear path off the beach."

Thinking back to the events of her day, Kate asked, "Have you met Mack?"

"Not yet." And then he countered, "I haven't received any special message either. From what I've heard, those are the steps that have to occur before you can get out of here." The volume in Val's voice noticeably began to rise. "Have you?"

"Yes, earlier this morning."

"And did you get a message?"

"Yes, that's the impetus that moved me to start the fire and use Ned's help to bring our beached peers together. I thought that perhaps we could all share what we know, connect with each other, and use that power to formulate our individual plans for getting back on the water."

"What was the message?" Val asked.

Before she answered, she became aware of a break in conversation within the group. She smiled, patted Val's arm, and stood up. Kate took the opportunity to introduce herself. Several sets of eyes turned her way.

"Hi, my name is Kate," she started a bit timidly. "I have something to share with you, something that happened earlier today while I was walking on the beach." She hesitated, took a breath and went on, "It was delivered as a sparkly message written on a brown paper lunch bag." She waited. No one laughed, no one gasped, and no one got up to leave. She continued, "It said, *Connect Deliberately*, and then it disappeared."

"That was the message?" Val interrupted. "Well, it's pretty obvious that we need to find a way to connect with a new ship and get back in the water." As everyone around the ring began to nod, the light from the fire sent their ghostly shadows up the face of the rock wall.

"I'm not so sure that's all of it, Val," Kate said. "I'm pretty sure it has something to do with connecting first with each other. As I understand, when we land on the beach, people tend to keep their intentions, dreams, and plans to themselves. They disconnect and stay that way until they get on their next ship. Sometimes people will network with each other, but only when they have a specific need or are in trouble. Real networking and real connections take commitment, repeated contacts, and a deliberate investment of time."

"What do you mean 'real connections'?" Val asked quickly, cutting off any other responses. "I've got more connections and social networks than I can handle. Phones, computers, handhelds, digital downloads have me overloaded."

Ned interjected, "You're right. Sometimes I think it would be great to have been a librarian so I could sort, archive, and efficiently retrieve all those contacts and information and jokes and references when I need them. Sometimes I wish I had the power that exists in those contacts and could tap right into the varied and unique experience in my friends' heads. If you take everyone I know and multiply that by everyone they know, that's a lot of available knowledge and associations. Just think how you could use that information."

Kate's eyes lit up and she jumped in, "You see, until we get out there and commit to making the time to *connect deliberately*, and authentically, we're just sitting on the sidelines watching page after page and comment after digital comment blow right past us. Until we again become real to each other, and not just another contact on a friends' list, we'll never know what specific nugget of information, advice or referral is out there, intended just for us. I've been surprised more than once when I sent an email, voicemail, or met a friend for coffee and ended up getting the right nugget of information, intended just for me, that changed everything."

"Oh c'mon," Val sighed, "I'll admit I want, and yes, okay, even need, information and contacts right now, but how can I be guaranteed that the person I'm meeting is going to hand over anything important to me? I see it as a tremendous waste of time. I really can pull this off and get on with my life and back into the water much better by myself."

Ned laughed, "It's not about the other person—it's all about *you*. Connecting is offering up who and what you know first. It's letting the other person in on who you are, what you believe, and what you want to become. Then listen to them and that nugget will come to you based on the framework you crafted and sometimes when you least expect it."

"Wait a second," a voice from across the ring piped up, "isn't successful networking and connecting all about getting to know the other person first? How can you help when you don't even know where they are and what they need? Networking is like a spider web; fragile looking on first glance, but ounce for ounce, stronger than steel and incredibly effective."

Ned responded with a nod, "Hadn't thought about it in those terms, but I guess that real networking is a true back and forth expression of trust, regardless of who goes first."

Kate thought back to the seagulls. Watching those silly birds compete for food raised the possibility that by simply and deliberately connecting, each would have gotten a piece of the action and a share of the prize. Those were only birds, these are people who can help and support each other with very little risk and the potential for lasting personal relationships. A true web of trust with the potential to grow stronger and stronger.

Kate continued, "In business, we compete in our own departments for the best positions, then we compete between departments for the best funding and finally we compete between ships for the best customers, recognition and revenue. By connecting deliberately, starting right here, we begin building the bridges that will enable us to get back in the water quicker. Then what if we continue really connecting, who knows how our lives and the businesses we join will be affected for the better?" Kate let her voice trail off as she picked up a stick and began poking at the fire.

"It's all about give and take, regardless of what brought you here. There really is strength in numbers. But you have to get out there and work it." Ned added. "Sitting at your computer and tapping keys is not enough."

Kate turned and met the gaze of a young woman sitting a few places over who spoke up, "Sitting with my handheld is safe," she began. "It's easy digitally partying with friends because you can keep things light. The tough stuff, the really personal thoughts are more difficult to share. I dread asking for help and dread even more admitting I'm alone and scared. I'm ready to hear about other ways to connect, even if it is a bit risky."

Val stood up slowly, turned to a man in jeans on his left, extended his right hand and said quietly, "Hi, I'm Val Parker. My whole life has been turned upside down. Has something like this ever happened to you—and how did you handle it?"

Kate watched as conversation erupted around the fire ring. She realized if this had been a company water cooler, break room, conference room, or happy hour gathering, business cards and handheld databases would be spilling out everywhere. The mad information acquisition scramble would have begun. But here, on the beach, there were no cards, no handhelds, no smartphones, no suits, name badges, or titles to act as screens and barriers. Here, people simply *connected deliberately*.

Kate sighed in peace at the end of this day. Tomorrow would be here soon enough and she felt armed with a new outlook and a few new connections to meet it head on.

Five

Pearl pink clouds crept up the horizon signaling the approaching arrival of the new day's sun. Low tide waves lapped softly on wet sand. The stillness was deafening as if the world was holding its breath in anticipation.

Jan glanced at the abandoned fire ring remembering last night's gathering. She was comforted by the variety of stories she heard and new introductions. A partially burned stick from last night's fire made a great stylus as she traced 56 over and over in the sand, deepening the indentation with each stroke. Her mind wandered back to events of the past month. He was too young to die. Now she was alone.

She tried to forget the morning paper left askew on the breakfast table, obituary page open, and the words highlighted in yellow: "*…long-time resident, served on local community boards. Survived by his loving wife, Jan.*"

With a lump in her throat, Jan let her gaze travel over the landscape, turning from her scribing at the fire pit to a line in the sand down the beach. The pounding force of last night's high tide had rolled up on land, stretching to reach as far as it could before retreating. The shells deposited by the waves looked like a handmade necklace against an unspoiled sand canvas. Marveling at their precise and perfect placement against the contour of the sand as far as she could see, she wondered, *Was this really the work of the pull of the moon, or was it just the ocean's way of making contact with the land?*

Walking up to the line, Jan picked up a large orange and white shell and put it against her ear. There was comfort in the memory of childhood beach outings. Her mother's whispered words were as near now as they were then, "Ask a question from your heart and then listen for the answer from the sea." Jan was pretty sure there wouldn't be any answers coming from this shell or from the sea today.

She was aware of how her thoughts tangled in her head like the seaweed at her feet. Thoughts of the fire ring, new friends, his death, the now distant dream of retiring, and the overriding, *now what?* Having been married for the majority of her adult life, Jan admitted her world and her aspirations had predominantly revolved around him. Early years of struggle, building their life in the small town, and working their plan to retire within the next couple of years had been her focus—her happiness.

She wasn't prepared for this. Their ultimate dreams and goals had been close enough to touch before doctors and hospitals took over. Remembering their early years in the family business; grueling hours on the manufacturing line, regulations and distribution processes, shipping and receiving, and his steady climb to supervisory, management, and finally executive roles. There had been no family nepotism here. They worked hard for the life they wanted.

Often standing for hours by his side, she knew the whine and whir of every machine; when they were working well and when each needed attention. Her life without him was broken. The reliable sounds of the well-oiled machinery had fallen silent.

With the bulk of their social and work life revolving around the company, Jan's acquaintances and friends had come and gone through the years with the cycles of business and time. It broke her heart to think of the impact on each of those people as they heard the news. She wondered where some of them were now. She longed to see those familiar faces.

Beached. She regretted having lost touch with so many of them as she brushed at the tears rolling down her cheeks.

The horizon came alive with rush hour on the water. Jan appreciated the diversion. She was amazed that even without painted lines or traffic lights, ships and boats were able to get in sync and avoid crashing into each other. Oddly, that thought had never crossed her mind while she was on the water, bouncing from commitment to commitment with her head down in a range of daily tasks. The beach provided an interesting external perspective of that activity and motion.

With no particular destination in mind, she let her feet guide her, one step in front of the other. First down to the water's edge and then back to the shell line. The variety and mystery of the shells reinforced her sense of awe at the power of high tide waters. Large clam shells mingled comfortably with small mollusks, sand polished mother-of-pearl, and interesting bits of coral dotted the shoreline with color and texture. She was fascinated by how the line could be completely random yet predictably placed. *Magic,* she concluded. The thought of something magical in this situation raised her spirits for the first time this morning.

Shell after shell, ribbons of seaweed, and scampering crabs helped to click away bits of time as she strolled. Jan momentarily became intrigued by what she thought was a pattern against the sandy backdrop. The shells seemed to have been picked up, one by one, spelling out words. Inquisitively, she glanced around and saw that hers were the only footprints in the sand. There, clearly spelled out in shimmering shells reflecting the sun's rays were the words:

RETHINK YOUR WAY

Jan stepped back to take it all in. *Who did this?* she wondered taking a step closer.

"Greetings," an unfamiliar voice traveled over the breeze.

"Hi," she responded, turning to face him. Jan didn't remember him from the fire ring last night and struggled for a moment to recognize his face.

"Did you do this?" she asked, pointing to the shells.

"I think that's the work of last night's high tide," he proposed.

She looked back to the shell line, observing only the random scattering of shells tossed by the tide. The message was gone. Her heart raced and she felt a little dizzy. *Am I seeing things?*

Taking a step closer he said, "I'm Mack. I'm the lighthouse keeper. Would you like to sit down?" Glancing over his shoulder, Jan thought it odd that there were no footprints logging his path in the wet sand.

"Thank you, but I think I'm going to walk down to the water for a moment. I've got to collect my thoughts. I think I'm seeing things."

Shore birds ran up and down in the low tide feasting on scurrying sand crabs. Gentle tide waters splashed repeatedly over her feet and ankles. Jan's world had been so predictable until his passing. Funeral preparations and final goodbyes had given way to messages in the shells and people who walked without leaving footprints. She wanted to curl up in a ball and disappear.

Sitting comfortably and appearing to enjoy the warmth of the early morning sun on his face, Mack greeted Jan as she walked toward him.

"Welcome back. Perhaps you'd like to sit a moment," Mack offered.

`Still feeling wobbly, Jan nodded and eased down next to him on the sand.

"Isn't this a beautiful morning?" Mack asked. His words floated easily through the air and delivered a comfort that Jan hadn't felt in weeks. Sitting deliberately upright she tried hard to let his words and the peace of this moment seep into the sad and cold places in her heart.

"I used to love the beach in the early morning," Jan offered. "All previous traces of yesterday washed away leaving promise and hope. New and untouched possibilities like a fresh canvas waiting for us to paint the picture of our day."

Mack smiled stretching his legs out in the sand. "And what would you paint today?" he asked.

Jan paused, thought for a moment, and then began, "Well, the picture of what I believed my life would be has vanished. My best friend is gone. On top of that, the piles of sympathy cards remind me one by one of cherished friends and family who have moved far away and out of my life. My dreams and goals feel like broken glass at my feet." Mack didn't respond choosing to let the resonance of her words drift silently on the breeze.

Several long minutes ticked by before Jan offered, "So I'd probably start by painting that shell line." She paused with a frown. "Although I don't know if I would even begin to know how to paint those shimmering words." Her voice drifted off as she suddenly realized that she hadn't stopped to consider what *Rethink Your Way* meant for her.

Mack picked up a small rock and threw it into the surf. "What if I asked you to paint your dreams now?" he asked.

"My dreams now?" she countered. I'm not sure I could. I always thought I knew what I wanted and was clear as to what it would take to get there. Now I'm here and I haven't got a clue what to do next."

Pointing to the sunny cliff above them, "It appears my immediate plan to end up there with the man I love is shattered."

Mack shaded his eyes looking at the retirement community up on the bluff, high above the beach. The homes dotting the edge were just coming to life. The crisp whack of a golf club teeing off the first ball of the morning echoed against the cliff. Mack knew many of the residents in the community, having met them through the years when they were beached.

Giving Jan a nod Mack went on, "Those folks put in their time, met the challenges life presented, worked hard, and made the decision to reside up there as the next chapter in life. They spent years on the water exploring their talents, interacting in communities: selling, servicing, sharing, earning and spending, learning and teaching. Retiring was the next step, not necessarily the realization of a predetermined goal. Some moved to different careers, different dreams—and some may still be working to make their happy ending come true."

Shifting his gaze to avoid the direct sunlight, "There is certainly more than one goal, however, and the way to find it is to tap into previously unconsidered dreams. Sounds like this particular goal and dream of yours was all planned out," Mack observed.

"Well, of course," Jan answered. "Everyone knows about the sweet life of the retirement village. We worked hard to plan for our own well-deserved retirement lifestyle."

Mack scooped up a handful of shells. "You've collected the shells of your life, your memories, and your accomplishments like a well-feathered nest egg. You've mastered the challenges of the tides with your ever increasing responsibilities to your family, friends, and community. The line you've drawn for yourself in the sand outlines your desired and potential long-term dreams. Just like the high tide, you appear to have positioned it all so intentionally. Why would you abandon it now?"

"Abandon it?" Jan admitted her temptation to set it all aside and give in to the heaviness and paralysis of futility, fear, and overwhelming sadness.

A small sand crab dashing across the seaweed diverted Jan's gaze. She watched it head toward the shell line and wondered if the goals and dreams she had been hanging on to for so long would be strong enough to carry her, alone, into the future? She needed a dream to believe in and the courage to get it going. Shell-lined words stating *rethink your way* swam before her eyes. *This doesn't make any sense.*

"Could you see that shell line when you were on the water?" Mack asked, interrupting her concentration.

"Not really," she said. "I never actually thought about it."

"Look out at those boats in the water," Mack directed.

Jan watched the commotion on the horizon confirming that it looked choreographed, as if an unseen director was telling them where to go, stop, and turn.

"Can you see inside? Can you tell me what everyone is doing on those ships?" he asked.

Jan thought a moment, "No, but I can guess what they might be doing. It's not the same as being on board. Each ship has its own mission and different people have unique jobs to make it happen."

Mack let her words settle in before he continued, "It's all a matter of perspective. Your dream belongs exclusively to you. It's as unique as the example of those ships you mentioned. The trick is finding your personal joy in creating and realizing that dream. You get to choose your way with every new day as you create each new shell line."

Glancing upward Mack shared, "Everyone up there on the bluff found an individual way to make his or her dream happen. Some paths were quite direct while others meandered like the shell line. Some paths were smooth and seemingly effortless, while others were filled with potholes and speed bumps that delivered weary travelers, battered and bruised, to their home on the hill. And while individually they might not be totally happy with the path they took; ultimately they've come to realize the value in each choice, each fork in the road, each detour, that helped them realize the fulfillment of their ultimate destination, whether the bluff, the beach, or the water."

"I wish I could be as sure about my way as the tide was when it captured the shells and drew its line in the sand," Jan sighed.

Mack laughed, "Do you think the tide cares whether the shell line tomorrow morning is lower or higher than it was today? Do you think it cares if it draws a line at all?" With that Mack stood, picked up his walking stick and began to step away.

"Wait . . . please!" Jan pleaded. It was a knee-jerk reaction. She really had no idea why she asked him to stay. "Then, what does the tide care about?" she called out.

Mack raised his hand in farewell, and without turning around said, "It cares about doing what it loves to do."

With that, Jan watched Mack walk toward his home. On a narrow point of land, a solid sentry stood tall against the dangers of the jagged rock and explosive surf. Brilliant skies and cotton clouds framed the laquered black roof of the lighthouse. Blasting through the prisms in the turret, the sun sent rainbows splashing on the green hillside behind.

What do I love to do? she repeated. Years with her husband had brought satisfaction and the means to a life she enjoyed. Remembering long days at work, business trips, and the rising cost of stress increasing year after year, contributed to missed time with friends and family. Where had it gone? Why hadn't she paid more attention? Regret growled like a small beast in her heart.

Today, being beached, gave her the time to rethink. Concerned well-wishers standing by couldn't be expected to define her path, or the resources she would need for the upcoming journey. It was up to her to consider ways she might take to realize a new dream—all the while doing something she loved. Settling into this new perspective, she decided it felt good. Conscious of the sun on her face and wonderful memories beside her, she gathered as many shells as she could. This was the first step on her own and she intended to capitalize on it.

Six

Hearing distant voices Jan turned and spotted Val shouldering a heavy wooden plank. A group of five or six others circled in discussion and pointed at some sort of drawing in the sand. She watched for a moment as Val set his plank down and pointed to something in the center of the circle. Heads bobbed with lively conversation. As she walked toward them she thought about Val's notable reaction to Kate's and Ned's dialogue at the fire circle.

For the last couple of weeks, Jan had pegged Val as an independent. She figured he was someone who would use his determined will, his intellect and his experience alone, to get back in the water. She even felt he might channel the anger and hostility he felt about the hurricane toward shepherding his family to safer ground and stronger shelter. She didn't see him as a *connect deliberately* kind of guy.

"Good morning, Jan," Val called out. "Want to join us? We're hoping to cast off just as soon as this last plank is in place."

Jan could see now that all the activity pointed to the development and outfitting of a rather fine looking catamaran. It looked to be strong, stable, and well equipped to launch this group back in the water.

She questioned where it had come from as Val chatted excitedly with the team.

"How did you all build such a sturdy boat?" Jan asked.

Val slapped his hands together to dislodge the wooden slivers and sand. "It didn't take long after Kate shared her message for me to realize that I didn't have to do this alone. I've met lots of people during my time on the beach but hadn't bothered to really get to know anyone or acknowledge individual strengths. I left the fire ring and began to connect, one by one. Everyone wanted the same thing and we discovered that with our combined skills we could make great headway. By working together, and more importantly, continuing to *connect deliberately* and find the missing talent we needed yielded these terrific results. I don't believe we would be as far along if we had tried to do it alone, or worse, competed against each other. There really is plenty for everyone." Jan thought back to Kate's seagull story and the forsaken lunch.

Val fiddled with a compass, "I guess I was pretty busy feeling angry and resentful at being beached. I know my anger caused me to isolate myself. Now I see that I really do have control of my destiny. I just needed the help of a network to guide and point me in the right direction. Are you ready to join us?"

A ray of sunshine reflected off the shiny brass compass causing Jan to squint. She glanced back to the lighthouse and thought again about her conversation with Mack. Her perspective had indeed changed. The potential for a new shell line—a new goal—was intact. She only needed the time to rethink the way she was going to make her dreams happen.

As her thoughts converged, she was sure about one thing—she still wanted the dream she had envisioned. Get back in the water, work hard, engage with her dear friends and family, and make it to that elusive bluff and community overhead. However, the path would be different than what she had previously planned. Clarity came as she decided to take this time, stand back from her personal shell line, her past accomplishments, her dependence on her beloved husband, and find out what really would enable her to define happiness and a new path. She wanted the chance to do what she loved to do and find a way to turn that into a successful acquisition of her dream. This was the time and place to figure out exactly what that meant and then define the course, and the ship, to get there. She wasn't sure what was next, she just knew it was not the right time to get back in the water. She hadn't yet found her compass.

She wished Val and his team a profitable journey. While they might not understand her need to stay, she knew they would respect her decision. Reuniting with the mantra *rethink your way*, in her head, she set out in search of more clues.

Seven

Jan searched up and down the beach, in and out of vacant shore caves, going from tide pool to tide pool, not even really sure what she was looking for. With a tangle of relentless thoughts in her head she was happy to let the day unwind as she sorted through the storm of options and new ideas. She couldn't wait to share with the others her mysterious message and newfound perspectives. The fireside discussion would surely help her crystallize next steps.

Walking with a sense of determination, Jan let fresh paths and exciting possibilities explode across her mind like fireworks. She could see the light from the fire ring dance up and down the rock cliff. It blended with her flashes of accomplishments, memories, and promises inviting her closer. She turned from the water's edge and joined others now making their way to the designated ring.

Familiar faces greeted her with a mixture of friendly recognition, acknowledgement, and even some, she thought, with an inquisitive glance. She knew she felt different but was it apparent? Grabbing an open spot near a couple she met several days ago, Jan easily settled into the evening's event.

Once the sun dipped below the horizon, a chill blanketed the beach. Directing her gaze into the dancing flames, Jan recognized the dual pull of the fire—attention, care and feeding in exchange for welcoming warmth. *It's impossible to have one without the other,* she thought. *Just like the attention, care and feeding required by my dreams and goals.* Staring into a fire brought a comfortable dreamy space. Jan let her mind wander at will. Dreams and goals spun in her thoughts like wispy webs against the background of the dynamic flames, neither one standing still, each just out of reach. *How am I supposed to hang on to one goal long enough to map out a plan to achieve it?* She allowed herself to envision the potential down the road—a year from now perhaps. The whirling eddy in her head was beginning to slow down some, but she still couldn't make out a solitary, clear goal. Belief in her abilities and courage to try a different path was getting stronger. The path she would choose would ultimately have to be up to her, along with the accompanying rewards and consequences. Her perspective, her vision, her determination would be the tools to bring her dream to life.

"Jan?" The voice seemed to come from the center of the fire. A hand on her shoulder broke her train of thought and she looked up to see Kate standing next to her. "Are you okay?"

"Everything is great!" Jan replied, eager to share what was going on. "You've met Mack, haven't you?"

"You bet! What a remarkable fellow. Our conversation lasted only a short while, but the impact on my thoughts has been profound," Kate responded. "And you?"

"I met him early this morning. We talked about perspective and ways to achieve the goals I want for my life, or at least what I *think* I want for my life." Jan patted the vacant rock next to her, inviting Kate to sit.

Kate watched Ned poke at the fire sending sparks flying into the inky night sky. Jan tracked several sparks until they flew out of sight. It was time, she decided, to reinvent the way she would feed the fire of her dreams.

Familiarity with each other and the fire ring protocol led conversations to be more muted than the initial animation of last night. The snapping of the fire and the drone of the waves mixed with quiet voices, provided a comforting stage from which Jan decided to share her thoughts with the group. Standing, she met several upturned faces and anticipatory smiles.

"I'd like to share an interesting message I received today," she started softly.

"Go ahead," Ned invited. He balanced his descent onto a large piece of driftwood across from them, settled in, and watched as everyone else put conversations on hold to listen.

Relating the adventures of her day; finding a message in the shell line and meeting the lighthouse keeper, held the group's attention. When a waver crept into her voice, she consciously upped the volume before stating, "The shells spelled out the words *rethink your way.*"

Her eyes circled the group and she watched as the words resonated with some but connected with all in the group. She couldn't help but wonder what each of them, individually, thought it might mean for them.

As high tide began rolling in, waves gained strength and crashed with a persistent roar onto the lighthouse rocks. Winds gently teased the fire's flames pushing them first one way and then pulling them back. In spite of the warmth of the fire, Jan felt a shiver tap her back.

Gathering a new resolve, she continued, "I know that being here is probably not what any of us had planned. It certainly interrupted the path to my dream. And yet, the time we've been given on the beach has already impacted the way I look at that dream and my planned way to achieve it. My perspective has changed. My solution will have to change too.

"I believed that if my husband and I studied hard and worked our way up the ladder of success we would be rewarded with retirement and family and friends to share it with. The tide has turned and that road has been washed away. Now I have to rethink each step in front of me. It isn't easy." Jan sat back down but no one broke the silence.

A stack of wood, sheltered by the cliff wall, seemed to be growing day by day. Everyone knew the fire ring provided more than just warmth at the end of the day. Ned reached back to grab a gnarled piece of driftwood and lean it on the edge of the fire.

"What do you really want?" he asked.

Softly, she answered, "I want to see beyond the end of the beach or the edge of this sadness. I want to be able to plan a course that will ensure the same happy ending that we had planned. Life has provided wonderful opportunities and we loved meeting them together. Now it's up to me to continue our business and maintain our home. Our business was the driver of our goals. We deliberately settled for the sacrifices that accompanied the advancements and new territories. When promotions were linked with raises, we met the challenges head on and didn't step back to ask if the new position would make us happy or help us be the people we really wanted to be."

"I know what you mean," Ned added. "Sometimes it felt as if I had sold my soul to those business drivers. And while I often questioned myself about choices made, in the end it was as if I had traded my real dreams for titles, money, or power. I guess I always thought I could make time to pursue my dream and that elusive happy ending later on."

"We all have a path not taken," Kate added. "Circumstances of our lives and our responsibilities sometimes require us to make difficult choices." She thought of the Confucius saying, "Choose a job you love and you'll never have to work a day in your life." But, she cynically wondered, who really was able to do that?

Ned looked up at the stars. "I believed there was some great master plan that was plotting out my destiny and guaranteeing the benefits I sought. Crashing on the beach made me realize how foolish that was. I now realize that I'm the only one truly responsible for creating my happiness. My best guess is that all those highs and lows along the way reflected the company's dreams and not my own. And while I may not have immediately realized the monetary benefits of acting on my own instead of being attached to the company, I'm convinced that in the long run it all would have come out the same. He paused briefly before adding, and I probably would have been happier."

Jan exclaimed, "That's it! That's what I'm after. I want to feel at the end of each day that I have reached and realized my own happy ending." Grabbing a stick at her feet, Kate and Ned watched as she judged the middle and then successfully balanced it on her index finger after only two tries. Setting it down again on the sand, she continued. "I'm constantly balancing fear. I wake up at 3:00 a.m. panicked at the thought of having to do it without him—having to do it alone. What if I fail? What did he take care of while I was doing the other half of the balancing act for our business and our home? How do I position my life now against potential threats and simultaneously ignore the insistent roar of having to do it single-handed?"

"The tough part is trying to figure out what it will cost you," Kate said. "Everything costs something; money, time, energy, or passion.

How will you balance the dream you are living with the dream you want to realize?"

Ned excitedly jumped in, "I think it's coming clean with what you have to give up. Perhaps I won't get the gold watch at my retirement party that I've had in my head for years. I may have to give that up. I may have to let go in order to live a little more deliberately and share precious happiness with those who are important to me, every single day, without waiting for corporate promises."

"But have you considered what might be there for you when you let go?" Jan asked. "I realize I've been holding on so tight, making sure that every morning that line in the sand that defines what I have accomplished thus far is exactly where it should be. I've been too scared to even consider what might happen if I didn't hang on to that dream and to the path we laid out to get there. Mack told me that the tide cares about one thing: doing what it loves to do. When the tide recedes every morning, that shell line is there for everyone to see. Then the tide is free to go out and create something brand new. I want that freedom and that joy."

Digging her toes into the cool night sand Kate began to whistle softly as her eyes traveled from face to face around the ring. Messages, Mack, conversations, and new connections battered around her brain. Val used the message *connect deliberately* to join with others and was now back on the water. With contagious passion, Jan shared her message, *rethink your way*, and certainly seemed to be doing just that!

Yet, here she sat. Adrenaline butterflies in her stomach signaling a peculiar mix of confusion and anticipation. Had the message seen on the brown bag and shared with the group actually been intended for her instead of Val? *What's next*, she wondered. Since shedding her high heels and suit coat on the driftwood, the weariness of the search for answers and a path back to the water weighed heavily.

Spirited banter tumbled around the fire ring with stories becoming livelier and richer, as confidence and familiarity among the participants grew. Jan's eyes sparkled in the light. Oversized gestures punctuated her dialogues and while Kate couldn't hear specifics, she would catch Jan's laughter over the din every now and then. It made her smile.

"So, what's next for you, Jan?" Kate asked. "What does your new path look like?"

Jan stopped and briskly rubbed her hands together. Kate wasn't sure if she was trying to warm them or if, like a happy child, she was signaling glee.

With tentative excitement in her voice, Jan answered, "I've never had time to reconsider the purpose of everything we accomplished thus far. This is that moment and even though circumstances pushed me into it, I'm nonetheless going to take it with gusto. This beach, and this time have given me an opportunity I haven't had before. I want to see where my shell line will be tomorrow morning, and the morning after that. I know there are no guarantees. I just know that I'm going to reach out and accept the love and support around me and then let it guide my path to my own happy ending. I'll do it for us both." Brushing tears off her cheeks, Jan let her voice trail off as she sat back focusing again on the flames.

Eight

Every day on the beach was responsible for its own concert. On some days the strings and woodwinds carried the melody down the rocks and over the dunes where whimsical sea grasses danced and waved in appreciation. Other times the brass stepped forward and proclaimed the majesty of the noon day sun with a clarity that pulled all manner of brass instruments to join in. Today belonged to the percussions.

Thunder cracked overhead and a gray fog hung low over the damp beach. The normally frenetic seagulls huddled together in anticipation of rain. Blasting a throaty groan, the foghorn warned water travelers, while on the beach a metal trash can lid banged against a nearby drain pipe. Waves collided against the shore gathering power and becoming louder with each crash.

Spence watched the rhythm of the waves. Mesmerized, he drifted uncomfortably back in time to the moment he was called in to the CEO's office. Standing up from behind his polished mahogany desk, he stopped to straighten the framed photo of his beautiful family. Angry gray-green clouds signaling an impending storm that day put on a spectacular show from his fifty-second story window. He was proud of everything he had achieved. This office, his title, and staff were the payoff.

Unprepared for the CEO's opening; Spence sat down hard on the leather couch after hearing the first couple of sentences. *"Spence, you know how valuable this company thinks you are. The Board of Directors and I want to take this opportunity to thank you for your exceptional service in getting us through the merger. However, hard decisions had to be made. We are confident the next company that benefits from your experience will provide new challenges and opportunities for you."*

Both Spence and the CEO jumped involuntarily as a flash of lightning and crack of thunder lit up the office. The memory brought him back to the beach with the thought, *how did this happen to me?*

Droplets of rain pinged on a nearby metal hatch cover washed up on the sand. Turning his face to the sky he welcomed the rain. Being a realist, his job now was to confront where he was and what he had to do next. He surveyed his surroundings while considering his fate.

Spence had always loved the beach. Growing up near the ocean gave him a chance to master all forms of body and board surfing. Statewide and even some national trophies and medals attested to his competitive success. Stormy weather didn't bother him. Rough water drove outstanding wave height, and it was too tempting to resist today, even without his custom board or flippers. Raw body surfing would have to do.

Running as fast as he could and diving head first into the water, he surfaced several yards from shore. Assessing his position, he adjusted his feet in anticipation of the next big wave. Readying his body like a weapon, he planned on piercing the apex of the breaking wave becoming one with the force and direction of the water and riding it to shore. He waited patiently for that perfect combination of maximum height, depth, and strength.

Wave after wave, ride after ride, he performed flawlessly. Breathing hard on the shore, he stood, turned, and swam out to even deeper water. With a clearing head, Spence reflected that he had been riding the unending variety of life's waves since he was little. He was good in school and even better playing basketball. Scoping out the currents and the riptides of life, he knew who to ride with to help him catch that next wave, and who to leave behind when he was being dragged under. Success, with accompanying rewards, depended upon his sharp instinctive focus and reaction to water conditions, weather, and available tools.

A small back wave curled up, lapped against his chest, sprayed water in his mouth and caused him to cough. Distracted, he failed to prepare for the gathering wave behind him. Climbing higher in its imposing force, a commanding wall of water smacked hard against his back. Tumbling wildly and bumping hard along the sandy bottom, he struggled to gain his footing. The weight of the water buckled his knees, carried him to shallow water, and pushed him face down on the shore. Sputtering and coughing salty water while gasping for air, he slowly regained his focus.

Sitting up and not knowing whether to laugh or cry, he looked to see if anyone had witnessed his crash. Brutal memories came to life in his head carrying the uproarious laughter and pointed fingers from high school buddies who surfed with him. When one of them fell flat and missed a chosen course of action, the rest never abandoned the opportunity to heckle. This time, though, the miss seemed more serious.

Here he was, sitting on a beach exhausted and frustrated, instead of waiting behind his desk for the next crisis, the next opportunity to shine. The script had been laid out so well: high school advanced classes, scholarships, college basketball championships and corporate recruiters. Coveted success through consecutive promotions generated a boxful of accumulated business cards and shiny brass name plates. Heralded as the next "up and comer" he admitted his naiveté in believing the corporate media hype.

He let the thread of memories continue, again feeling the flush of pride and the sense of having truly arrived when he saw "Vice President Sales and Marketing" on the door of the newly designed and decorated executive office. With a view of the city below and a staff that turned his departments' visions into profitable realities, he was secure. He never expected the merger that seemed so exciting less than six months ago would send him sprawling here—beached.

Lying back on the sand, he cupped his hands under his head and let himself go limp in submission. Movement near his head caught his peripheral vision and he turned his head to see jet black eyes of a tiny, resident hermit crab meet his gaze.

Rolling away from the little guy Spence sat up to get a better look. He remembered reading that hermit crabs traveled in packs as they scavenged the beach. More crabs equaled more available shells. As the shell of a big crab became too confining, it would be abandoned for a roomier one. The discarded shell would become the new home for a smaller crab that would happily leave his cast off for the next crab and so on and so on. Fog swirled in around him and the analogy wasn't wasted. He felt like a crab without a home; vulnerable, sensitive, and scared.

The crab began to crawl away. *Only one hermit crab? There should be more.* Curiosity drove him. He stood up, turned his back to the waves, and began searching for more crabs. Symmetrical tracks in the sand indicated the crab's journey along the water's edge. Not wanting to disturb the activity, he was content to hover at a distance watching several busy crabs in a variety of sizes. Speed was not their forte, but deliberateness in their movements appeared to yield, for some, a new home. What was the protocol for abandoning a current home and staking claim to a new one? Was it like musical chairs? When the music stopped, what if there was no shell to climb into? It must take courage to climb out on the sand without protection or a defined destination.

Wanting a better view of the crab village, Spence chose a dry spot uphill and lay prone with his head on his hands. A spunky little crab went from shell to shell in search of a new home. He found some shells already occupied while others were summarily rejected. Spence watched the crab's pursuit in wonder. What made one shell right and another one not as good? The shell exchange process was intriguing.

Aha! The little crab apparently found the ideal shell. It wasn't the one that Spence would have chosen; neither as colorful nor as shiny as some of the others. Nonetheless, once the little crab was comfortable in his new home, he headed straight for Spence's nose. Stopping within inches, he peered out with pearl shaped, intense black eyes and in a rather large voice for such a small creature said:

MAKE WISE DECISIONS

Startled, Spence stumbled backward using hands, elbows, knees, and feet to gain his balance. He landed, instead, squarely on his rear. Wild flailing limbs and flying sand caused the group of crabs to scatter under rocks, burrow into the sand, and scurry to the water's edge. The lone little crab, however, stood his ground.

Spence stood up and briefly considered this might all be an apparition and not real at all. He looked down at the crab and simultaneously considered getting back in the water. Stalled low-hanging clouds and a thick fog bank rolling in from the sea determined his decision to stay on dry land. Brushing a combination of wet and dry sand off his skin, eyeballing the lone crab one more time, while attempting to quiet his now shaky legs, he resolutely walked away from the whole scene. *Encounters with talking crabs would make anyone uneasy,* he concluded.

He couldn't help a final look over his shoulder to see the crabs regrouping and resuming their house hunting activities. He longed for purposeful activity and was glad that none of his friends could see him now. Feeling unsteady and a bit bruised from the morning's events, as well as unproductive and somewhat embarrassed at being beached, he scoured the horizon for anyone he might know.

In the distance and through churning fog, he watched the shape of a person materialize as the distance closed between them. It reminded him of a Polaroid picture developing before his eyes. Bent over an unidentifiable stack of something on the beach, Spence could make out a man in pants rolled to his knees and a baseball cap. Slowing his pace and with his guard up at the possibility of encountering a beachcomber, he considered his options. When he was a kid he thought that being a beachcomber might be a great way to live. As an adult, he knowingly categorized beachcombers as needy, lazy, and shiftless drifters with great addresses, but not worthy of invested time. Ignoring the internal warning to turn around, he surprised himself by accepting the strong pull to keep going.

"Good day to you," said the beachcomber.

"Oh, yeah, same to you," Spence answered without making eye contact intending to brush past the man.

Now closer, Spence validated worn and rolled beach pants and a hooded gray sweatshirt pulled close to keep the damp day out.

Beached

Mack was clearly embroidered on the left front. He stole a sideways glance, mentally filed his name, and would have been happy to keep on going.

"Quite a morning," Mack commented looking at the clouds overhead. "So much to hear in the wind as it travels by, and sometimes from local shelled residents—if you are really listening."

Spence, while momentarily intrigued, was content to ignore the comment and let the conversation drop as he stepped back from the remnants of a broken wave.

"Been surfing long?" Mack asked.

"Grew up with it," Spence answered.

"So, big waves and unpredictable currents don't throw you much, do they?"

"I don't know. I guess not." *Where had this guy been watching me from?*

Spence thought back to those big waves, unpredictable currents, and raging storms weathered over years in the corporate world. Where did he miss the road signs that would have warned him to play the merger cards differently? Being beached was the wave he never saw coming. Sarcastically he thought, *maybe if I play my cards right now I could be a drifter too*, as a smirk crawled across his face.

"Frankly, I don't think you have what it takes," Mack said.

"Excuse me?" Spence stopped and looked back at Mack. Instinctively he set his stance as if he were waiting for the onslaught of a wave. He was already feeling miserable with a fuse that was getting shorter by the minute. "You haven't got a clue what I'm capable of!" he fired back.

Pulling the sweatshirt hood off his cap exposing the logo of the lighthouse, "I'm Mack," he said. "I keep watch over the lighthouse and if I'm not intruding, I'm pleased to make your acquaintance." Mack tipped his head slightly to the right and gave Spence a silly crooked smile as he observed, "Your attitude has you wrapped pretty tightly today."

Just when Spence thought he couldn't feel any worse . . . he did. His quick assumptions were based on old biases and maybe even a bit of fear that he might be on the road to becoming a drifter—and worse, invisible.

"Sorry Mack, I really didn't mean to take my life out on you. You want to talk about big waves and unpredictable currents? I rode the wave of success right here to this very beach." Spence stamped his foot hard on the wet sand. "And now I haven't got a clue what to do next. On top of that, I'm being given advice from a hermit crab."

"Is the advice worth taking?"

At that moment Spence realized he hadn't given the crab's words much thought. Allowing his mind to wander, he recognized that many of the decisions for his life: the right school, the right college, the perfect girl, the best job, the next promotion, the next city, the next challenge and even the merger, had been made by someone else. And while he believed those had all been his decisions he now wondered—*were they really*? His doubts were as heavy and gray as the clouds overhead. His future seemed trapped in fog and he felt powerless.

"And so?" Mack pursued the original question. "Is the advice worth taking?"

"*Make wise decisions*," Spence repeated the message. "I honestly thought that I had."

"And just when was it, before now, that you felt as vulnerable as your little shelled friend?"

"Truthfully? Never. I don't even think I would know how to look for the next shell. It feels pretty hopeless." Spence had never heard himself sound this defeated and found it alarming. He picked up three rocks and flung them one by one, as hard and fast as he could, into the foamy white-capped water. He wished that would have made him feel better, but it didn't.

"Everything you need, to find the success you are looking for, for the rest of your life, is right here on this beach . . . right inside of you," Mack said confidently.

"Oh, c'mon," Spence snapped in exasperation. "I don't hear headhunters or powerbrokers in country clubs, cigar bars, or board rooms calling my name or sending me offers here on this beach."

"That's pretty limiting," Mack observed. "You'll never know what marvelous ideas, what outrageous unlimited possibilities can occur until you are willing to abandon the protection of your old shell and struggle to find your new best fit. You only truly own what you deliberately choose and consciously struggle to have. When you are small, you can only carry a small shell. If you choose one that is too big, it will crush you. Take the time to find and carry the shell that fits. The carrying will help you grow."

"So, if this beach is my shell for now," Spence asked, what do I do next? I feel like I've turned the next page of the script for my life and it's blank. There are no directions. I'm feeling exposed and vulnerable."

"That's okay," Mack said zipping up his sweatshirt and pulling the hood back over his baseball cap. "Use the beach. Don't miss the gifts that are here to lead you to your next opportunity." Whistling softly, stick in hand, conversation finished, he touched the bill of his cap in a farewell gesture, and walked away.

Spence felt like he was seeing the beach for the first time. A switch had been flipped on and his senses were filled with sights and sounds that he hadn't even been aware of, until now. He wanted to see, and hear, taste, feel, and know it all.

Sprinting up to a nearby vacant swing set he settled onto the rubber seat, grabbed the chains and began pumping furiously, rising higher and higher. Ocean landscape was being unwrapped bit by bit as the sun burned through the fog. Even the fog horn had stopped. Rather than feeling empty and vulnerable he now embraced the burning in his leg and arm muscles pushing himself in this childhood activity he hadn't done for years! His breath came in uneven gulps interspersed with abandoned laughter. Dragging his feet to stop the motion, he dropped in a heap on the sand. He recognized the same sense of disorientation inflicted by the wave that dropped him during his earlier surfing escapade. Only this time it was welcome.

The light broke through and the warmth of the sun's rays enveloped him. He opened his eyes to see a crystal blue sky breaking through. Getting to his feet and tying his sweatshirt around his waist he started to jog down to the water's edge. With nothing particular on an imaginary to-do list, the running became like a steady drumbeat urging him on . . . to where? He had no idea, but somehow, that was okay.

Nine

Looking up from her sand castle construction, Jan spotted Spence running on the beach. She shouted and waved as he got closer, "Hey, Spence!"

"Hey there, Jan," Spence slowed his gait and turned up the beach to greet her.

The now bright sun made the sand and shells sparkle on the battlements of Jan's castle. A deep, even moat surrounded the castle's exterior. Spence wondered how effectively, and for how long it would be able to hold off the impending and inevitable, high tide.

The castle was impressive. A delightful variety of rocks, beach glass, driftwood, and shells indicated windows, doors, and an intricate courtyard, facing the sea. Reaching upward, majestically sculpted turrets suggested hidden rooms and secret spaces. Half expecting to see a tiny princess emerge and wave to him, Spence gave a low whistle of appreciation, "Wow. That's quite a sand castle."

"Thanks," Jan answered without looking up. She appeared to be putting some finishing touches on a side window.

"Are there dragons or royalty inside?" Spence inquired.

Furrowing her brow and sitting back on her heels, she considered

Spence's question. "I suppose I ought to have thought about that before now. If this castle is the representation of my life I guess I should know who lives inside and how that defines my role."

Interrupting her construction and with a pensive quiet in her voice she went on, "Protecting the castle had always been my husband's job. Right now, with his death, I'm envisioning some fierce dragons living inside." Images of their last months together, piles of spreadsheets, medical reports, and the non-ending stacks of hospital bills flashed in her mind. "I'm not really sure, but I'm scared enough of the possibility of their fire-breathing wrath that I don't dare build a door into or out of the castle without having my protection in place. I hate the thought of meeting that fire-breathing encounter.

I suppose I've spent years as a sentry; standing guard with a watchful eye, for both the dragons and my king, continuously shifting the priority of my vigilance for the protection of the castle and its future."

Spence watched the fog roll past her eyes just as it had rolled off the beach earlier. The light broke through and she said with visible determination, "I live in that castle now. Out with the dragons and hail to the memory of the king! I live in this castle with the royalty of my dreams, my own generated power, and a new path created to make it all come true. No telling what I'm going to find, I just know that I am going to open that door, without fear, and follow my heart."

"That's the spirit! You are creative, it's a beautiful castle, and it fits you well. Too bad it won't be here in the morning." Spence knelt down to peer inside one of the windows.

"That's exactly the point," Jan said. "I don't need permanent ivory towers to guard my dreams or protect me from my dragons. My perspective has changed and it's time to open the door and say goodbye to being held captive by my fears. My course has always been about being protective and overly conservative. Being beached has given me the perspective to realize the strength of my own capabilities and begin moving forward from there."

"But what if . . ." Spence hesitated. He matched Jan's smile and realized that she had described a place with no better or worse vantage point—no asset or liability—no plus or minus. It was all about consciously crafting a path that was uniquely yours and built from the resources close at hand. Like the tide laying down the shell line of today's accomplishments, making them as real and beautiful as possible; and then, if tomorrow brought a change of course, or washed the shell line away it would be okay. Every new day brought with it the opportunity to reassess challenges and goals with equal respect, rethink the way to make accomplishments and dreams come true, then delight in new perspectives gained.

Spence knew Jan had found the perfect start to *rethinking the way* to her dreams. Build a castle, acknowledge the gifts of the shell line, and employ the lessons from the sea. Five yards from the waterline and the sand was too dry to create a castle. A yard from the water and the sand was too wet, the waves too threatening and unpredictable. Today's best construction site might be under water tomorrow.

"Enjoy, Your Majesty," he offered as he bowed slightly and handed her a particularly beautiful piece of conch shell. Stepping toward the water's edge, he added, "I wish you the best," unsure whether she had heard him or not.

Turning momentarily, he watched Jan use the shell and carefully craft the wide front door. A smooth piece of driftwood became the drawbridge across the moat. With the iridescent shell line extending out on both sides, Jan's castle and its resident monarch were open for wonderful opportunities and possibilities.

Ten

Whitecaps dotted the horizon as a stiff wind picked up against the shore. A slow moving barge labored inch by inch down the watery lane while spirited motorboats darted across its wake. Stately sailboats with colorful jibs full of wind, glided silently by in teams of four. Spence felt his previously acquired upbeat mood sinking with the setting sun. It had been a good day and yet he was still here . . . on the beach . . . without obvious possibilities for returning to the water, and a new job.

Leaning back against the rock wall he allowed the stored warmth from the afternoon sun to radiate across his shoulders. *Make wise decisions,* he thought. *What are my options from which to make those wise decisions?*

Drifting back to the idyllic, carefree days before a job and family responsibilities dominated his world, he closed his eyes and remembered bonfires on the beach, roasted hotdogs and cold beer, volleyball games that continued until it was too dark to see, and that miraculous first kiss from a sun-drenched girl with golden hair and long legs.

He opened his eyes just in time to see the last orange sliver of sun dip into the sea. The brilliant afterglow in the clouds and the lingering haze of his daydream merged. Like a bank of disappearing mist, he tentatively began to gain some clarity. He pulled his sweatshirt over his head and started toward the evening's fire ring.

With sluggish steps in the clammy sand, Spence consciously took time working his way to the fire ring. The excitement of the previous conversations and participants had changed. Val and his team completed their raft and were back in the water. Jan found a clear peace and was using it to guide her new path. They both seemed sure, determined, and happy. He felt caught without a job and worse, without direction. What was the value of sitting with these beached peers tonight rehashing the day?

Make wise decisions rang in his ears. *Should I stay here, or should I go to the fire ring? Which is the wise decision?* Amused, it occurred to him that just a few days ago he was taking direction from the board of directors and CEO. Today he was considering the advice of a crab!

"Grab a few logs there, will you?" Ned gestured with his head to the stockpile. His arms already loaded with wood.

"Sure," Spence replied. *Too late to turn back now.* He picked through the reserve wood pile looking for several sizeable logs dry enough to burn. Throwing them into a second pile, he was pleased to hear them crack as they hit the ground, indicating the sun had done its job. Grateful for a task that made him feel useful, he smiled and thought *this was a good choice, a wise decision*. He was appreciative of the singular focus of this work. The storm of emotions brought on by the day's events flooded his consciousness. Struggling to corral the feelings gripping his chest he became aware of the mix of exhaustion, excitement, and awe overtaking him.

Huffing a bit as he moved the wood, he mentally listed an hour by hour itinerary of the day trying to make some sense of it all. Surfing the morning waves, hearing the hermit crab speak, and encountering Mack all seemed so far away now. The strength and determination in Jan as evidenced by her castle bolstered his reflections. Sunset's orange glow with its inviting last light, presented an amazing visual gift. Now this wood would give warmth to end the day. Responding to a new lightness in his step he shouldered several substantial logs and moved more quickly toward the fire ring sensing that somehow the pieces were all beginning to fit together. He supposed that regardless of the decisions made here, on the beach, they didn't have to be cast in stone forever. "Flexibility" and "temporary" were definitely new concepts when applied to decisions for his own life.

The true power of choice and wisdom must not be taken lightly, he decided. Real wealth had less to do with money or possessions and more with having the choice, and the freedom, to make those wise decisions. This was a new way to measure his life. Options he once judged to be permanent were actually more fluid and flexible than he believed. Critical to making wise decisions was the infusion of his own wisdom and experience, elements that had previously been minimized in his decision making process.

"I saw you body surfing this morning," Ned commented, interrupting Spence's thoughts.

Spence chuckled, "Yeah, until I took a nosedive and washed up on shore." He decided to continue sharing and added, "I even came eye to eye with a hermit crab—a talking hermit crab at that!"

"Nice," Kate laughed. "What did the crab have to say?"

Dropping the log onto the fire, Spence sat down next to Kate. "The crab said, *'make wise decisions.'*"

"Sage advice from a tiny source," Kate said. "However, choices and decisions appear rather limited when you're beached."

"I thought so too," Spence went on, "until I realized that the real choices are the ones inside your own head. Henry Ford, the great car designer and manufacturer once said, 'Whether you think you can, or think you can't, you're right.' External scripts guided my entire life. The power of my own deliberate decisions in the opportunities or obstacles placed before me became secondary."

Smiling, Kate observed, "My favorite children's book was about a little engine that kept repeating to himself, 'I think I can, I think I can'… and in the end he did it. So what's next for you, Spence? What are the wise decisions dancing in your head?"

"This time I know it's not only about hard work, determination and profit. This time it's about making choices for me and then accepting, and even enjoying, the personal struggles and accountability that come with them. That's the key to my true wealth."

Dark pounding surf, to others may have seemed menacing, ferocious and impenetrable, but Spence saw something different. There it was and his for the taking; swirling tides throwing white-capped waves of potential new ventures, struggle laced with possibility.

It was at that moment that Spence knew it was time to get back in the water.

Eleven

Cold, wet, squishy sand oozed up between his toes and then released with a rude sucking sound as he placed step after step on the ground. Ian recognized two things he loved most right now—the colorless landscape of the beach before the sun splashed color all over it, and the fine line between dry land and the tide. Step too far to one side and water penetrated pant cuffs. Step too far to the other and there was nothing but boring dry sand. In the middle was that gooey mixture that made him feel good—powerful even, without having to give into either the capturing water or settle for the monotonous and uninspiring beige flooring that went on forever.

"Morning," a committed runner uttered with scratchy reserve breath as he passed by. Barely raising his hand in acknowledgement and feeling an overwhelming, unwelcome sense of intrusion, Ian immediately lowered his head, crossed his arms across his chest and turned back to the safety and solitude of his cave.

There was a universally acknowledged rule on the beach. Those who found a place of refuge and chose to close out the world of beached peers were left alone. Caves available both along the shore and in nearby canyons, rustic forts constructed as makeshift shelters, and pieced together tree houses scattered inland among the sturdier trees had been used by a variety of beached inhabitants. When Ian found this carved out rock face, he staked his claim and deliberately "went dark," pulling his emotions and his communication in with him. Like a bear in hibernation, he didn't need or want anything—or anyone.

Mack was the only one that Ian had allowed, albeit unwillingly, to impose in his space. Talking briefly on one of the first mornings of his arrival, Mack gently but definitively helped Ian understand the rule. While neither Mack nor any of the others would intrude, Mack and Ian agreed on signals by which Ian could communicate both his wellbeing or need-for-help status. "It just lets me know you are okay." Mack explained. Ian agreed to Mack's request without further conversation.

Days slipped into weeks. He had deliberately stopped counting and tried desperately not to care about the passage of time. That single innocuous measurement carried with it too much pain, frustration, and futility. What he thought was just an annoying bump on the back of his arm was now officially labeled as cancer—the Big C—he was an official member of the cancer club. Familiar rockets of anger flashed up the back of his neck and exploded behind his eyes. There was nothing he wanted or needed from anyone here on this stupid beach.

A heavy, dripping fog blanket hung across the cave's opening as the gloomy afternoon gave way to promise of a miserable night. Thunder crept up the beach ricocheting from one cliff face to another. Waves crashed and hissed relentlessly but the normally clear view of the water was completely obscured. His whole world was gray. Color left a long time ago.

Swallowing hard, and sucking in the fog, he choked back tears. Having been through every negative feeling imaginable since landing on the beach, he settled now for defeat successfully suffocating any semblance of light, external or internal. Grabbing his damp blanket he methodically pulled the edges around his shoulders edging as close as reasonable to the cave's small, sufficient fire.

It seemed to him that everyone he had come in contact with since leaving the water had unseen powers to dictate the path of his life and he hated it! Who were these people in lab coats and soft-soled shoes with authority but without a semblance of authenticity or compassion? Their litany of rehearsed phrases, "I'm sorry to have to tell you this. This won't hurt a bit. You can expect results within the next three or four days. We can only give you a best guess of the prognosis," left him dangling in the soggy antiseptic air like a lifeless puppet.

An unidentified and unwelcome harbinger of fate had chosen him. He now considered himself a mutant. At this very moment his body was producing tumor cells jumping into that perfect internal transportation system, his bloodstream, looking for a comfy spot to reside and begin growing anew. Cancer. It was real now, with a direction of its own, and his life, or what he had left of it, would never be the same.

The same as what benchmark, he wondered? Whenever in his life were there a series of months, weeks, or even days, when he was the same? The human body regenerated itself constantly. New cells, new thoughts, new perspectives with each day—some okay and some trash. What was that old adage, "You can never step into the same river twice?"

Everything changes with each moment that passes. New water flows. He just wanted it all to stop long enough for him to see the road ahead, choose a different vessel, make a different choice, or take a different route. *Ah yes*, he thought, *the infamous road not taken*. But this time the choice was obviously no longer his. Thrown on a route that wasn't even on his map, he choked on the weight of the medical albatross he now carried. Everything was an effort; each breath, each step, each word, and he didn't want to hear one more story about how this was the best thing that could happen to him.

A shower of sparks burst from the fire into the darkness. One small ember landing on his leg, caused him to jump back, drop the blanket, and hit his head on a protruding rock. Every curse word he knew boiled up from his toes and detonated against the cave walls. He had never felt so bruised, helpless, and alone.

Two resident seals barked back from the beach. He couldn't care less. Instinctively grabbing one of the last three fire logs from dry storage, anger prodded him to look for something to pummel. However, the remaining vestiges of good sense urged him to stoke the dying fire instead. Survive first . . . then go beat something.

# Twelve

Not wanting to add insult to injury by blasting his eardrums in the confines of the cave, Ian stomped outside into the open, wet darkness. Screaming at the top of his lungs he did his best to expel the bottled fury from every fiber of his being as he competed with the raucous thunder. Arms outstretched under the blanket of night where no one could see his antics and impose their judgment, criticism, direction, or attempt at comfort, he just kept yelling over and over. Gulping in air to fuel the repeated outbursts, he closed his eyes tight and stumbled in aimless circles, focused only on getting his internal dashboard to read "empty."

Finally, with only a whisper of a voice remaining, soaking wet, and exhausted, Ian dropped to his knees on the sand and sobbed. *Why me?* The question that had been tearing at his insides since hearing the diagnosis surfaced; the act of asking so pointless, time spent in the search for someone with a realistic, concrete answer so wasted. He was starving both physically and emotionally. Everything felt shattered and worn through and he had no idea what to do next. Cold pelting rain covered every inch of his body and ran in rivulets down the sand as he pulled into a tight ball, head on his chest, arms locked around his legs, shivering violently.

Surprised and momentarily confused, warmth and softness descended, engulfing him completely from head to toe. He immediately recognized the familiarity of a dry blanket and automatically pulled it tightly around him wondering, at the same time, if he were dreaming. The feel and smell reminded him of those special occasions when his mom would tumble the fleece afghans in the dryer and have them ready, tender and cozy, for his brother and him to snuggle into after a frosty afternoon of sledding.

Two white tennis shoes on the sand in front of him indicated a visitor. Clutching the blanket up for fear of getting it wet, he stood and faced the owner of the shoes. Recognizing Mack he muttered something about appreciation. Mack nodded and stood back, intentionally giving Ian space.

The folds of the blanket were generous enabling Ian to envelop his body once around and then pull it up and over his shoulder like a pancho, complete with a makeshift hood. His shivering subsided. Staring intently but comfortably at Mack he suddenly realized that Mack was completely dry. Not one drop of water from his cap to his shoes.

Ball lightning moving across the water and out to sea lit up everything in its path. Rolling flashes of light caught Ian's attention as the thunderstorm continued around them. Pelting rain had given way to gentle, but persistent showers. *We're not wet.* Looking up he saw clear skies and brilliant stars directly above them. He was convinced, however, that if he put his hand out beyond this arid silo it would get soaked. *What's going on here?*

"Shall we go back inside?" Mack asked gesturing in the direction of the cave.

Struggling still to orient himself after the events of the last little while, Ian looked around fearful he had travelled quite a ways from the cave opening.

A loud crack of thunder roared above and Ian watched as a new downpour dumped buckets of rain all around them hiding familiar landmarks. Unsure of his bearings, Ian was hesitant to take a step in any direction. "It's okay," Mack assured him. "Our path is dry. Just step out and you'll find your way. I'll be right beside you."

Step by step under solitary clear skies puzzled Ian as he headed toward the faint light of the cave opening. Relentless rain fell around them and yet it was as if an oversized, transparent umbrella protected their walk. Glad that he had stoked the fire before departing, he was grateful for the cave's warmth and light as they entered. Battering the world outside, torrential rain masked the view of the beach beyond his door. Astonished anew at his own dryness and comfort, he carefully took the blanket from around his body folding it slowly as he realized that absolutely nothing on him was wet. *I should be soaked.*

"I don't have much to offer you in the way of beverages," Ian said to Mack handing him the folded blanket. Mack stuffed it into his backpack.

"No need," Mack answered, "I'm okay for the moment. May I sit?"

"Of course." Ian followed Mack's lead, sitting down on a nearby rock aware of both the cracking fire and splashing rain. Neither he nor Mack spoke for awhile letting an easy and comfortable peace settle in.

Minutes felt like hours when soothing, relaxed conversation finally began, encapsulating them both. Ian drank it in with a thirst that astonished him. After several rounds of topics, peppered with personal stories and laughter, Mack asked, "What do you think people really want of each other?"

Ian sat for a moment contemplating the question. Unable to come up with an answer he felt was worthy, he countered instead, "With your experience, Mack, what do you think?"

Mack offered, "I think we want others to see us while we are here and miss us when we are gone."

"Regardless of the relationship or the circumstances?" Ian asked.

"Regardless," Mack answered soundly.

"And when I'm gone, who will really care?" Ian questioned uncomfortably.

"Who do you list in that authentic handful of people that you expect to really care, those who accurately see you—inside and out—regardless?"

Staring at the glowing log in the fire Ian again considered the question. He wasn't a kid anymore and his cache of family and friends was full and interesting—but authentic? *Strange word.* "I'd have to give that some thought," he decided as an appropriate and truthful response. Memories of family reunions and boisterous holiday gatherings flooded in. His internal movie continued running on to long-haired, tanned beauties, first kisses, lifelong buddies, and work friends.

"Recalling them in the albums of your mind can you see the connection that draws you together and the joy that fills the space around you? That doesn't happen with casual relationships." Looking directly at Ian, Mack shifted his posture until he was aligned with Ian on opposite sides of the fire.

Returning Mack's gaze with a calm ease, Ian felt an unusual power in the alignment. *I wish I could just be in this peace and this power forever.*

"Both peace and power are available for you, Ian. Take the time to really see those who are an authentic part of your life. Allow them to really see—and genuinely connect with you. Draw from their calm, their joy, and their power. It is there you will find your own power."

With that, slinging his backpack on his shoulder and standing, Mack touched Ian's shoulder and slipped gently into the night.

Dulled and battered as if time spent on the beach had done its best to beat it into either submission or extinction, an old spyglass lay on the rock where Mack had been sitting just a moment ago. Picking it up and turning it over in his hands Ian couldn't help but let his love of pirate stories influence his excitement at this unexpected find.

I wonder if he meant to leave this behind? Not much would surprise him at this moment. His newfound connection to Mack assured him that all was right, just as it was. Stars sparkled in the totally clear sky drawing Ian out of the cave with the telescope in hand. Moving away from the light of the cave to the isolating blackness of night, he put the glass up to his eye expecting to see stars pulled in close enough to reach out and touch. Taken aback, however by the distortion in his view, he used his sweatshirt to gently clean off the exterior lens. His hope was that the interior glass had not been cracked through years of use, making the telescope inoperable.

Satisfied with his cleaning efforts and grateful for the now clear skies, he returned the spyglass to his eye and tipped his head back for maximum target access. Again the clarity was masked, but rather than attempt another cleaning, he twisted the eyepiece as far as it would go and blinked in amazement as clear bold letters appeared in the viewfinder:

CHOOSE TO SEE

With his mind racing in an attempt at clarity and with the spyglass cradled safely but gently in his hand, he looked out at the horizon. Illuminating the straight black line between water and sky, a bright orange slip of the rising moon broke through. Training the telescope on the horizon, Ian somehow knew the words would be gone. And they were—transferred from the glass into his mind and heart.

At that moment, he knew he was now less satisfied with fleeting, tangible answers and more determined on a quest for lasting peace. By truly seeing his own circumstances, emotional reactions to them, and the love of those people provided to give him support and strength, he would find the answers and that lasting, if not elusive, peace.

What moments before had been damp and cold was now surprisingly as comfortable as a balmy summer night. Ian sat easily on the sand taking his sweatshirt off and carefully laying the spyglass next to him. With deliberate purpose he rubbed the bump on the back of his arm, "seeing" it through touch, for the first time in months. *This belongs to me and I have the power to take the next steps and see the path ahead, authentically, for what it is.*

Picking up the spyglass, Ian pulled the stars around him like a dazzling electric blanket. Exchanging bitterness for hope and emptiness for warmth, he allowed the punishing weight of the last several weeks to drift away. His focus now was the promise of a rare, delicious sleep filled with peace and dreams.

Thirteen

The new day dawned as bleak as Kate's spirits. Shivering in the morning haze she tried hard to make sense of it all. The life behind her, the beach this morning, her future, high career hopes temporarily dashed, and most importantly her inability to control any of it lay mixed in shades of sandy gray at her feet.

The messages, the fire ring, the new friendships all meant something, yet, she missed the comfortable rhythm of the work left behind. Work demanded everything she could give with a dependable and satisfied exhaustion waiting at the end of each day.

Here on the beach with no responsibility and little accountability as the primary engineer of her time, she constructed her own agenda. All she had to go on, so far, were stories of incoming messages, a soggy brown bag, and the challenge to try and apply it all to her time here. Unfortunately none of them were fitting very well. With that gloomy thought, she plopped down on the sand, happy to watch the morning dance of the sandpipers.

Up and back, up and back, advancing and retreating with the early tide moving along the shoreline, pecking furiously at the sand, these spry little birds appeared to be enjoying their tender sand crab breakfast. Unlike their obnoxious neighbors, the seagulls, these lithe spirits were not tempted by human crumbs and leftovers. They weren't into begging. They were focused and careful in using the time given to accomplish survival tasks.

Action in the water diverted Kate's attention from the shore. Surfing the dark and ominous morning waves, she saw Spence enjoying riding in, paddling out, and riding in again. The repetition reminded her of the sandpipers.

Traveling high and being carried far with a serious potential for crashing was built in to every attempted ride. Was it the sense of danger that separated man from the sandpiper? Was it tempting fate that provided a sense of excitement?

Riding the last wave all the way to shore, Spence moved away from the water's edge and collapsed on his back. Approaching him quietly, Kate inadvertently scattered a small flock of sandpipers in her path. Breathing heavily, Spence lay on the sand, spent from his adventure.

"Are you okay?" she asked.

"Never better," Spence pushed back with the remaining air in his lungs.

"Sucking wind and unable to move, you could have fooled me," Kate jabbed. "Mind if I join you? I'm tired of the gloom in these overcast mornings."

"Really?" he asked with surprise in his voice as he sat up. "I hadn't noticed. These are the kind of days that provide opportunity for great wave rides, unexpected challenges, getting back in the water, total exhaustion, and the clear thinking that comes along with them all."

Kate poked at a ball of kelp, with her finger. Eagerly waiting for the day's sun to warm her spirit as well as her bones, she scanned the landscape for light. Impatient to brighten up the beach in front of her, she responded "I know, I'm getting more eager, day by day, for my own great rides, unexpected challenges, total exhaustion, and clear thinking."

"Do you surf, Kate?

"I tried it a couple of times during family vacations in my teenage years. It went the way of most sports that might break a bone or two."

Spence laughed out loud. "I sure know what you mean. I can't remember the last time I surfed with such abandon." Tapping the side of his temple Spence added, "I know now that it is all about using the power of those waves to break out of the limits I built in my mind. Surfing represents for me a push beyond my self-imposed comfort zone. I want to challenge those limitations that I pulled in to protect myself. Being beached, and really seeing the lessons here, has given me the opportunity to step out of my comfortable shell and be vulnerable. Ever since my encounter with the hermit crab, I have become more observant of even the smallest details around me.

"My message to *make wise decisions* has given me a multitude of meanings. My life is more than the dictates of the corporate world. The high-rise shell they provided gave me an opportunity to grow and learn over time. The wise decision is to recognize when the shell becomes too small. I'm going to look for new challenges in unexpected places and if I crash along the way I'll pick myself up and get ready for the next wave and the next opportunity to ride with joy and abandon."

"Good for you," Kate offered with a slap on his shoulder.

Standing with a full-faced smile, Spence said, "Be well, Kate. I'm off!" And with that he dashed off, with a sleek dive, into the water.

Watching Spence master wave after wave, Kate stared until he had moved well beyond the breakers. She understood that like a kid in a candy store, Spence was eyeing his possible opportunities in the ships and boats in front of him. Maybe he would choose one today—and then again, maybe not. Regardless, she knew he was on his way.

Fourteen

Morning haze burned off exposing a crystal clear afternoon. Alternating between making a list of priorities and exploring more of the beach, Kate felt her temperament and heart rate leveling off. Invitations from new friends to join them had been respectfully declined as she found contentment in walking alone. A rough peninsula, extending out from the shore caught her gaze. She hadn't noticed it before and decided to investigate.

Getting closer, she was enticed by the aquamarine-colored rocks laid like an underwater mosaic across the shallows, stretching thirty feet or so offshore. With the low tide, she visually followed it out to a large flat rock.

Envisioning that rock surface spacious enough to hold a table and four chairs, she easily remembered adventures with good friends. A conjured mirage of food, cold drinks and conversations jumping from politics to family, to business and beyond, beckoned her to wade across the submerged path and relive the memory firsthand. Cool water around her ankles, low tide, and a bit of a quest were too much of a summons to ignore.

Surveying potential liabilities from her conservative and cautious side, Kate decided the worst thing that could happen was a rising tide covering the stones and with it, her walking return to the beach. If the tide ran high and the waters deep, she could certainly swim that far, if she had to. Likewise considering the potential assets to be gained from this adventure, she firmly planted her foot on the path, expecting it to be slippery but happily surprised to discover it was not. *Follow the yellow brick road,* she thought with a giggle, *lions and tigers and bears, oh my!*

Unwilling to trust the initial solidity of the path, she picked her way carefully across the wet stones. Within three or four yards of reaching the platform, the land behind and on either side of the mosaic path sloped away significantly and the depth of the water turned from sandy beige to midnight blue. As if her path was now floating on its own, she could no longer see bottom. However, it felt as solid as the dry land she had just left.

Arriving on the giant rock, she turned and took in the full expanse of the beach. The cliff above exposed several retirement homes close to the edge but its height and her vantage limited the view beyond that.

Amazed at how much larger the rock was in actuality than it appeared from the beach, she returned to thoughts of close friends and the camaraderie they shared. There would be so much to tell them when she saw them next. *If they could see me now! They really will never believe all this.* Deciding to visualize the party she would have, she mentally arranged a table and chairs and set out her favorite china. Centering an arrangement of roses and daisies, she chose matching placemats and napkins to reflect the blue and green of the rock, sea and sky. Next she considered the food that she'd serve, when a huge splash of water drenching the entire scene, startled her back to reality.

Soaking wet, Kate wiped her face with her hands and turned to confront the source of the downpour. Bright blue skies and calm seas indicated neither transitory rain cells, nor incoming surf, nor wind-whipped whitecaps. Without either a commercial boat creating unexpected wakes or errant rafts with pranksters in sight, confusion greeted her.

Another whoosh and a splash doused her again! This time, however, she saw the source. The lacquered black and pearl white hide of an immense Orca whale disappeared silently back into the water. Seconds later, a jet black dorsal fin rose majestically out of the water indicating the direction of his journey. Following the fin, she laughed at his now obvious antics and the ability to send plumes of water with a single flip of his tail. Thrilled to see one of these magnificent and magical mammals up close, she immediately and completely, discounted her soggy state.

Kate was pleased to see he was not alone. Mesmerized by young bulls repeatedly breaching with amazing force and then falling back into the blue-black water she marveled at the towering sprays of white foam chasing their exit. Their demonstration of power and beauty filled her completely. Farther out, she spotted the remainder of the pod. Several males flanked cows and calves, safely protecting the young and vulnerable. Completely captured by their presence, Kate allowed the rest of the world, along with her concerns and cares, to momentarily evaporate.

Sitting down comfortably on her rock grandstand, the magnificent whale performance captivated her heart. One after another they breached and slapped their tails on the surface of the water. Kate applauded and whistled appreciatively for several minutes, then felt a quick pang of disappointment as she realized they were swimming farther away from her rock. They were leaving!

One lone bull seemed to take up the rear herding the stragglers along. Watching him intently as he glided across the pod's departing path, she thought it unusual that he didn't immediately close the gap between himself and the rest of the pod.

Turning in a smooth, deliberate swirl toward her, Kate considered that he actually might be coming closer. Kneeling as near as she could to the rock's edge she held hopes of reaching out and touching him. With a solid stance and clear head, she was nonetheless caught by surprise as he swam and stopped within inches of her outstretched hand. Shiny opalescent letters against his jet black skin revealed a message like advertising on the side of a blimp:

CONTRIBUTE

She blinked in disbelief and when she looked again, the Orca had disappeared. "Thank you," she whispered. Her mind projected the solitary word in front of her, dancing effortlessly on the now still water like a mirage. She looked up and mentally pulled the vision from the water to the backdrop of the clouds. There it was again, this single word—clear, defined, and completely in her control. She played with the word for a moment, visualizing it first on the water, then in the clouds and finally against the sand of the distant beach.

With the whales gone and her party over, Kate was eager to return to the beach and share her message. The ocean's calm and the comfortable stone path provided an easy bridge back. Once on firm sand, she turned and instinctively waved in the direction of the departing pod. She had her message! The one she knew was intended solely for her.

Hints of orange and gold signaled the waning path of the sun, the end of the day, and the opportunity to share her message around the fire. Swinging her hands freely as she strolled up the beach, Kate let the word *contribute* roll over and over in her mind. A strange peace lingered in each part of her being.

Recalling the message on the lunch sack, and her reaction to it, she was unmistakably aware of the difference in the way this word made her feel now. This message was meant for her. This time she was not just the messenger. Ahead she spotted the familiar outline of Mack as he picked something out of a kelp bed and waded out in ankle deep water placing it carefully on the sandy bottom. Then back he went to the large seaweed bed to do it again. She picked up her pace to greet him.

"Mack," Kate called out resisting the urge to hug him.

"Hey there, Kate," he smiled generously. "And how are you on this fine afternoon?"

"Great, Mack, just great." Kate responded wrinkling her brow as he again turned to the gnarled, umber-colored bed searching for something.

"Can I help? What are you looking for?"

"Starfish, my dear. They get tangled in the seaweed as it makes it way from the ocean floor. They are doomed here on the beach without a hand to twist back the braided traps and help them return to the water." He gestured toward a bright blue one partially hidden under a large kelp bulb. "Pick it up firmly, but carefully."

Kate accepted the directive.

"Now, step into the water far enough out that the next wave won't return it to shore. The starfish will do the rest. They have a great hydro propulsion system."

Kate was sure this was more information than she needed, but following his direction she returned the starfish to the sea. As she set it down she was amazed at how vibrant the color had become under the water. *What an unexpected reward in helping this animal survive.*

"Contributing to the life of another is pretty powerful stuff," Mack declared.

Unflustered by his observation of her unspoken thoughts, she considered his statement. The word, *contribute*, was gaining momentum in her head like a snowball down a mountain. Kate remembered a definition that one that her favorite high school teachers had posted years ago—*Contribute what you have acquired, or contribute your own acts—you choose. But leave the world a better place for your having been here.*

Unconsciously, Kate began walking alongside Mack. Attempting to match his gait, step by step, she was aware of the perfect indentations her footprints left in the sand. Consumed by her message and the surprising opportunity to contribute, she felt grateful for the repetitiveness in the act of walking. Looking back at the kelp, the surf, and the line of footprints, she was momentarily taken aback when she noticed Mack left no footprints.

Before she could question it, Mack asked, "Where do you contribute and to whom?"

"Honestly Mack, I don't think I have ever given it much thought." Donating to church, The Girl and Boy Scouts, and local school events sure hadn't made her feel as special as the rescue of this solitary starfish.

"Well then, what is the difference between donating and contributing?" He asked, continuing his search for ensnared sea stars.

Feeling that there was something really important in that distinction, she began to sift and sort through the thoughts competing for her attention. *How do I really contribute to the lives of others? I'm confident in my business acumen, my creative ideas, my talents, and my willingness to share with others. I donate regularly—but contribute?*

Looking out at the calm of the ocean, Kate's pace slowed and a new calm began to fill her. The act of handing money over to a charitable organization, while valuable, was fleeting. Searching out and prioritizing those opportunities to really give of herself was currently lacking in her life. Perhaps this was the balance that her heart needed. Contribute would demand more from her. She supposed that her whole concept of what it meant to be a contributing member of her world was about to change.

Mack's bighearted laughter suddenly filled the space around her. Looking up, Kate saw a black and white Border Collie down the beach furtively grabbing at driftwood tumbling in the shallows. Noticing Mack and Kate she bounded toward them. Dropping the makeshift toy at Mack's feet, the happy dog shook her wet coat, sending a spray of water over everything in range. Picking up the stick Mack threw it as far as he could into the surf. And she was off in hot pursuit.

"Pretty dog, is she yours?" Kate asked aware that she had not seen other pets on the beach.

"She attaches herself to anyone who needs her here," Mack said.

Within a step or two he turned to Kate, "When you contribute, you give away a precious piece of yourself, your time, or your resources. You could have walked right on by that starfish. You had that choice. Had you donated money to an organization that saves starfish, you might have accomplished the same goal. Instead you contributed yourself. Donating is a one way action. Contributing is a dialogue. That starfish gave as much to you as you gave to him. As you balance the lives of others through your contribution, your own life finds its balance and you find your center."

An insistent bark punctuated Mack's last sentence. "This is our playtime." He tipped his hat in a gesture of departure.

"Wait a minute," Kate intercepted Mack's path, wrapped her arms around his shoulders in a bear hug and whispered in his ear, "Thank you, Mack."

Without further hesitation, a smile on his face, and a furry black and white friend by his side, Mack moved on to pursue wet, sandy driftwood games and search for the next starfish.

Fifteen

Dusk quietly descended in a velvet curtain of cooler breezes and the quieting of daytime clatter. Kate sought out the warmth and company of the fire ring. Anticipation in the presence of these newly acquired friends and great listeners gave her the opportunity to share her day while gaining additional perspective, feedback, and guidance.

As she approached, she discovered only a few familiar faces gathered around the dark, smokeless ring. Ned wasn't there. *Had he left the beach?* Realizing her dependence on the predictability of Ned's fire and the comfort of his conversations she momentarily readjusted her expectations.

Stepping toward the cache of firewood, she picked up an armful intending to initiate this evening's fire. Several hands quickly joined her efforts and happily she realized the evening had been launched. Comfortable chatter ensued and Kate's reassuring calm returned.

Captivated by the fire, Kate watched the word *contribute* surface and submerge in her mind like the remarkable whales had done earlier. Snippets of conversation with Mack ran like a sound track accompanying her visions and memories of the day. Relaxing into the evening and the mystery of the fire, she worked to internalize the connotations and value of this message in her life.

A quiet hand on her shoulder broke her concentration making her jump. "Good evening, stranger."

She turned toward the sound of his voice. "Ned! Where have you been?" Leaping to her feet, Kate grabbed his hands in hers.

"Did I frighten you?" He said, taken aback by her excitement.

"Oh, not at all," Kate responded. I received a message today and I'm eager to share it with you. And while I'm still sorting through what it all means, I'm looking forward to getting your feedback and using it to help me get back in the water."

"Well, whether or not you noticed," Ned continued with a teasing air in his voice, "I haven't done so well in getting myself off the beach. But if listening will help, I'm here for you." With that, Ned and Kate walked back to available seats nearby. Ribbons of light raced skyward as new tenders kept the fire well fed.

"So tell me about your day and your message," Ned prompted.

Careful not to step on the momentum rolling in other people's stories, Kate paused and dropped her voice just a bit. "I was visited by a pod of magnificent whales and one of them delivered the message *contribute*."

Stillness enveloped the group and Kate found herself the center of attention. "Contribute? That was all?" came across the circle.

"That and a most interesting conversation with Mack," Kate replied. "We've all gained so much from these evening groups that I wanted to share the message with you and then get your feedback and ideas about it too. What does the word *contribute* mean to you?"

As if a switch had been flipped, sharing, stories, laughter, and even a few tears erupted around the circle. Allowing herself to really feel this opportunity to contribute to the group Kate listened quietly to nearby narratives and responded to those that resonated for her.

Ned turned to Kate, "Most of the time at work, and home, I give it all I've got . . . and then some." As Kate nodded her understanding he went on, "What do you do with your very best? Your very best talent, your very best effort, your very best output, your very best meal, your very best outfit, your very best creation? Where does it go?"

Involuntarily pulling her eyebrows together, Kate mentally chewed on his question before answering. "I'd have to say my work and family first, and then the community around me."

Nodding, Ned went on, "We define ourselves by those things that we are best at. Yet those well-developed foundations of our lives, those anchors of our personal best, need to be deliberately given away without expectation of reward, for us to be considered true contributors."

Others slid into the discussion, "However, have you considered that giving away the best of you may leave you vulnerable, like a sea creature out of the water? What happens after you give away your best?"

Another added, "Have you ever found yourself at risk having given more than you think is comfortable and even, at times, safe?"

A quiet voice near Kate offered, "But parts of you open up only when those things you are hanging on to so tightly are given for the good of another, without an expectation of acknowledgement or return to you."

Ned added, "And what you get back when you contribute not only makes you feel great but adds so much to the strength and richness of your life. Contributing doesn't need to rule your life, but for me, it absolutely has to be a conscious and deliberate part."

The continuing din of conversation faded into the background as Kate's gaze returned to the center of the now blazing fire. Whales, balance, giving in dialogue—there was so much here to consider, integrate, and act on. Perspectives, like tectonic plates, were shifting in the center of her being. She was eager to contribute, really contribute, by letting go of fear of the unknown, lack of control, and need for personal acknowledgement. She had so much available to contribute to others and she was ready for the unexpected returns to her own life. Why had she been hoarding her best?

Clarity came slowly. *I need to reset the balance in my life. Maybe the drive to be needed and acknowledged should be repositioned.* She visualized the symmetry and beauty of the whales. Breathe and glide. She filled her lungs with a long, slow draw of cool night air.

Reaching in her pocket she handed the girl with the quiet voice a bleached white, coin-shaped sand dollar. "I found this my first day here. Sand dollars have always been one of my favorite beach treasures. Because they are scarce, and fragile, they are precious and hard to find intact. I want you to have this one."

Firelight danced in the girl's eyes as she looked at the prize covering her palm. Turning the sand dollar over in her hand, Kate's fireside neighbor offered, "While I would have loved to save this as a memento of my time on the beach, I know someone to whom I am going to contribute this precious shell along with an invitation to join us here tomorrow night."

"Good for you," Kate acknowledged. Standing, she first bid farewell to Ned with wishes for a good evening. Turning to the group, "I'm off to contribute the rest of my accumulated treasures. The weight of those acquisitions isn't necessary and certainly isn't worth carrying around anymore. I'm ready to trade control, fear, and uncertainty for balance in my family, my community, and my work." She moved away from the fire and into the dark night, her gait now taller and more confident as she glided easily along the sandy shoal slipping out of the fire's light.

Sixteen

Ned gave up his morning run on the beach, faced the water, and began counting out loud, "One, two, one, two, one, two," as he flung his arms up and down rhythmically doing wide jumping jacks. The motion, the numeric mantra and his pounding breath joined the tempo of the ocean and pulled at the anxiety in his gut.

Remembering those first days after the ship had crashed, beaching them all, he snickered at his then confident idealism. Cynically now, he recalled the interactions around the fire pit and stories about hidden messages and profound conversations with a lighthouse keeper. It was trying his patience and certainly testing his belief system. He trusted there was something about self-discovery to be learned on this beach. Yet he couldn't keep the seeds of doubt from sprouting like weeds and choking out the original enthusiasm he had shared with those who were now back on the water.

Watching others gain insight and move their lives along highlighted the futility of his previously well thought out efforts. He was still beached. Focusing on his absence of hope he was sure it existed in the aftermath of gaining a message and experiencing the beach's magic. Everyone else certainly seemed excited about it! The relentless passage of ships back and forth fell in with his counting and compounded his frustration.

"One, two, one, two, one, two." The pounding in his head coupled with the fatigue hitting his calves intensified rising anger. He was tired of regrets, wasted time, faded dreams, and broken promises. Hopelessness overtook him and he couldn't resist the impulse to strike out against it all. "I want my turn," he yelled into the morning wind.

Physically exhausted and mentally spent, he dropped to the sand hitting unexpected resistance where giving sand should have been. "Yeow!"

Pulling his knee into his chest he could see a deep red imprint and knew a nasty bruise would follow. Hurriedly pushing the sand away he uncovered a gnarled black rock. Picking it up he threw it as hard as he could against the cliff wall. Both his frustration and the offending rock exploded in pieces sending chunks of rock flying like a meteor shower onto the sand. Rubbing his knee with little regard for the insistent throbbing, Ned laughed at his immature behavior until his sides ached.

"That felt great!" he said to no one in particular. He steadied himself and appraised his knee when a bright glint of light hit him squarely across his eyes. Instinctively closing and then rubbing them, he opened to look around and locate the source. Splinters from the thrown rock mixing with dislodged stones at the base of the cliff wall sent shards of reflected sunlight in a wide arc. Shading his watering eyes, he focused on the base of the wall.

A sliver of silver peeked out of the sand. Curious, Ned stood and limped over to the wall. Reaching down, he swept at the sand to expose a lid of smooth, shiny metal. Repositioning himself between the metal and the sun to avoid the intense reflection, he continued brushing to reveal an old-fashioned metal box. Holding it carefully and blowing away remaining flakes of sand, it reminded him of an antique cigarette box that sat on his grandmother's walnut coffee table years ago.

Taking the weight off his knee, Ned sat down cross-legged in the sand. Savoring the moment, he carefully opened the box. The aroma of tobacco and the telltale brown crumbs confirmed his suspicion that indeed this had been used to hold cigarettes in days gone by. He reached inside for what he believed was one lone, remaining, dry cigarette.

Instead, a rolled piece of beautiful old paper; antique and probably expensive, but not quite as yellowed or fragile as he expected, lay framed against the aged wood. Balancing the box on his knee, he removed the paper and slowly unrolled it.

"Ned Buckingham," was centered perfectly in calligraphy script. The next line continued, "You are invited to be present" but below that, the paper was torn away.

Shocked, Ned blinked hard and read it again, "Ned Buckingham, you are invited to be present…" Present when? Present where?

Replacing the invitation in the box, and cradling it under his arm, Ned stood and backed away from the wall. If an event, a party, or a meeting perhaps, was happening here on the beach, someone must know about it. Momentarily thinking back to his desk at work, he longed for the electronic calendar that had run his life. His computer was the central communication center. He could have simply pulled up his email or calendar and every event that he needed to know about and everywhere that he needed to be would magically appear on the pale screen.

Completely caught up in the moment, his sore knee forgotten, he walked toward the water's edge, turned and surveyed the beach. Shading his eyes he let his gaze take in the view from shore to cliff top and from side to side, as far as he could see. Closing his eyes a kaleidoscope of colors and muted beach sounds enveloped him.

"Lost?" The question pulled Ned back to the sand with a figurative thump.

Pausing a moment to let body and imagination reconnect, Ned looked around slowly to see an unfamiliar face. But the description from others at the fire ring, and the insignia on his hat were consistent, "Are you Mack?"

Mack smiled with quiet concentration and extended his hand, "Yes."

"I am very happy to meet you, finally." Ned took Mack's hand in his and comfortably met his gaze.

Then in one smooth motion, Mack removed his cap swiping the top of his forehead with the back of his sleeve. Replacing his cap backwards he surveyed the beach from end to end and top to bottom, then turned back to ask, "What are you looking for, Ned?"

Did I tell him my name? Ned's fleeting thought gave way to the possibility that Mack might know where Ned was supposed to be. "Maybe you can help, Mack. I need information. It seems I've been invited to be *present* somewhere."

"Right you are," Mack nodded and winked.

"Where?"

With their backs to the surf and gesturing in a sweeping arc, "Look out there," Mack instructed. A solitary target immediately caught Ned's gaze. Soaring high above the beach, a lone eagle played with the wind, owning the sky.

"Beautiful," he whispered turning to Mack with an expectation of an answer to his previous question.

"You must be present to win," Mack continued.

Puzzled, Ned went on, "That doesn't answer exactly where I'm supposed to be." With a final, majestic circle the eagle disappeared into the clouds. "My experience, time, and energy are testament to the dues I've paid. I want to be present. I just don't know where. Can you help or not?"

Thoughtfully, Mack put an arm around Ned's shoulder urging him to begin walking. "You've worked hard through your life to ensure your future is secure. Maybe in your pull and push to control that future, you missed the best part. This present moment."

"Being beached? I want to get back in the game, Mack. I don't have to have a guarantee of success or winning. I can make that happen on my own. I just need to know where to be." Frustration and disappointment colored Ned's words.

"You hold all the cards, Ned. You define the game, you make the rules and you determine the course. The beach is more than a location; it is your state of being and your choices that determine if you win or not."

Crumpling his brow and feeling baffled, "The invitation asks me to be somewhere, at some time, but I still don't know where or when."

"Like the eagle, you've acquired experience and prowess to soar, see, hunt, and sometimes even defy gravity. You are best, Ned, when you are truly present. If that eagle's attention is diverted by the past, or pulled into the future, he risks a miserable and humiliating crash."

Stopping to readjust his cap, he picked up a new walking stick and turned to face Ned. "Now is the best time to learn about now." With a nod and another wink he stepped into the swish of a wave on the shore, passed Ned, and hiked in the direction of the cliffs.

Dumbfounded, Ned considered what just happened. Knowing, through his uncertainty, that claiming this moment as his own was the key. Remembering the box and its message still tucked carefully under his arm, he sat down. Gently placing the box next to him, he laid back, hands behind his head and watched his friend, the eagle, soaring again overhead. Like the eagle, the message, and Mack's addendum, dipped and soared in his mind you *are invited to*

BE PRESENT

Closing his eyes against the strong sunlight, thoughts came in and out like scattered seeds in the wind. Ned, however, refused to let them land in his consciousness unless they defined or observed or acknowledged this present moment. Seeds of doubt, despair, and anxiety about the future pushed hard to try and land without success. It was in the now that he began to understand. Now he felt truly present.

Seventeen

"Ned!" Kate yelled as she ran toward him. Ned shaded his eyes and looked in the direction of her voice.

"C'mon, c'mon," pulling on his hand, she coaxed him up to sitting. "What are you doing?"

"Enjoying the moment. Why are you so excited?"

Kate caught her breath, "Just when I think I've figured everything out about the beach, and my new friends, it's time to go." She gave Ned a wide smile.

"Are you getting back on the water?" Ned asked.

"I've made a list of everything that I can *contribute* to out there," Kate waved a piece of notebook paper covered with the curls and lines of hastily written notes. "It's amazing, really. I began writing down the things that I know I can do well and bring value to others. I started with one or two and then new ideas, thoughts, and previously unconsidered possibilities just began tumbling out. It was such fun that I moved to reflect on my life outside of the office." Without paying notice to the silver box, Kate parked herself across from Ned. Three piercing blasts grabbed their attention as two mammoth barges appeared to pass too close to each other. Turning back, simultaneously noticing the silver box and Ned's now swollen and bruised knee, Kate said, "Looks like you have a story of your own to tell."

"Admittedly, it has been a most interesting morning. But I want to hear more about yours."

Despite her concern for Ned, Kate eagerly went on, "Support and conversation from the group last night sent me off to take stock of my life, my acquisitions, and my talents. I started this list at day's end and continued when the sun came up. The strength and persistence of those whales kept me going.

Setting her papers down next to Ned's silver box and weighting them with a nearby rock, she continued, "I was sitting and writing when I spotted a bright yellow canoe with bold green lettering on the side sailing very close to shore. I waved to them and they turned toward the beach. I didn't know that businesses could access those of us who are beached. I was curious as to what they were looking for." Kate's breathing was finally returning to normal.

"If I hadn't known better, I would have sworn that they were actually looking for me. We talked for a few minutes and they were eager to know more about the list of competencies and accomplishments I was assembling. They shared the vision and mission of their business, and I *contributed* observations and considerations from my past experience." Kate's combination of tranquility and joy was evident.

"We spent time discussing current economic challenges and ways that some of my talents and time could help them in their new distribution business. I realized I have lots to *contribute* even if the opportunity isn't exactly what I thought I was looking for."

"Good for you!" Ned exclaimed. "Does this mean you have made a decision?"

"This is a chance to redefine what it means to *contribute* in my life.

I believe that this time I can give, and at the same time find the balance I need." She remembered a bumper sticker she had seen once: "He who dies with the most toys, wins." She smiled realizing how much that had changed for her now. She might create her own bumper sticker to say: "She who can give it all away, before she dies, wins."

"Oh," Kate said, "I almost forgot." With that, she reached in her pocket, pulled out a torn piece of paper and handed it to Ned. "Good luck, buddy!" Kate gave him a quick hug and dashed down the beach.

"The same to you . . ." he called out sending with her unspoken good wishes for her upcoming journey. Recognizing the fine quality and calligraphic style he had seen earlier this morning, he unrolled the paper she handed him and read aloud, "at the sailing of the schooner—*Adventurer*—today at sunset. Bring only your dreams."

Ned opened his silver box, pulling and smoothing the message, matching the torn edges and connecting the invitation halves. Perfect. *I believe I now hold the ticket to the next chapter of my life*, he thought. Brushing the sand from his clothes, he put the invitation away. Consciously determined to stay in the moment, Ned pushed the familiar urge to begin making lists for future plans, out of his way. Laughing and waving to the eagle overhead, he stood up and shouted, "Stay close, my friend! There are surprises on the horizon to share."

Intending to be able to account for each new moment, he took one deliberate step and then another. Complete in the wonder of the present moment and in calm harmony with the beach around him, he began the trek to complete the invitation and meet the *Adventurer*.

Eighteen

The big blue ship rocked gently as the flurry of activity dimmed with the setting sun and colleagues' waves of departure at the end of another long business day. Olivia's large glass-topped desk, while orderly, was piled with work undone, pending, or completed and not yet filed. In short, she remained overwhelmed. "Don't stay too late, Liv," her boss hailed as he sped past her door.

Olivia had been employed here for over seven years now. Sighing, she thought about her steady climb of promotions and responsibilities, the tremendous sense of satisfaction and pride, and with it the ever-present, accompanying exhaustion.

Having mapped a long-term strategy for their professional careers, property acquisitions, entertainment, investments, and dreams, she and her partner Jay were comfortable and content in their lives. A smile crossed her face as she thought about all they had wrapped around them and the joy she experienced simply being together. The ringing phone snapped her reverie. The caller ID flashed Jay's work number, but Olivia decided to let it roll to voicemail, and standing, chose instead to take a quick walk outside for a breath of fresh air. She'd return the call with a clearer head.

The range of oranges, yellows, and reds against the cobalt blue sky never failed to captivate Olivia's heart and soul. The promises of new day sunrises and the peace of day's end sunsets always brought her joy. Laying her hands against the teak and brass railing she allowed herself to be spellbound by sunset's fiery show.

Her eyes danced across the panorama, trying desperately to drink it all in, as the sun slipped from cloud to cloud on its path to the horizon's edge. She let her mind journey from Jay and home, to her friends, foundation and service commitments, vacation dreams, and finally here, to her job. She was content and yet she was aware of a small gnawing in her heart.

A bright beam of light flashed across the deck and pulled her gaze to the lighthouse and the beach. Remembering her own days on the sand, she watched as distant, unrecognizable figures moved about the beach.

Recalling confusion and frustration during what she now called the first phase of her time there, she was reminded of how angry she had been, trying in vain to find someone to blame for her beached and isolated fate. She laughed at the seeming futility of it all and realized how much she had learned about herself and her repeated yet unsuccessful attempts to control the future.

Most of all, she missed Mack. What a terrific coach—a true beacon in some of her darkest moments. His gentle wisdom and simple questioning even now gave her pause to reflect. She recollected her insistence on interpreting life in terms of tangible assets and assigning misplaced value to them. Without her important "stuff" at arm's length, without the security of ringing phones, meetings to attend, electronic messaging to answer, and piles of files to action, Olivia had been left available to receive and internalize her own valuable message.

What might Mack say to her now? What message would he ask her to ponder? She closed her eyes and visualized him walking toward her with his signature cap, sandy cuffs, and weather-beaten walking stick. "Hey, Mack," she whispered into the wind.

Clearing her mind she considered that being beached is not something to be conquered once and chalked off the list of life. Been there, done that. So many friends, family, and colleagues lived their life doing whatever they could to avoid being beached, and yet, there it was—and often over and over again. *Strange,* she thought, *some people I know are actually good at being beached.* Illness, work issues, family problems, tragedy, accidents, and even death burst through the safety of front doors and rattled the structure of life. Was there a secret to getting through it?

Olivia opened her eyes to see the last splash of sunset's colors fading into the dusk. A glow from the current beached dwellers' fire ring lit welcome memories in her mind. Recalling those lively conversations and shared messages took her to an oft forgotten space and time. Rubbing the lacquered teak of the ship's railing she realized the gnawing in her heart as a faint longing for those trying, yet precious days spent on the beach. Never had she been so close to the rawness and the simultaneous depth of her feelings. Never had she gained such clarity for the positioning of her goals and the required perseverance to see them through.

Persevere. The last message from Mack was so complete, so unceremonious, and so clear. She had used that single sheet of fine linen paper received from him as a treasured bookmark and daily talisman of direction in those early weeks and months on her new job. She wondered if she could even put her hands on it now.

Olivia took a final breath of crisp ocean air before walking back to her office. On the bookshelf to the left of her desk were treasured tomes, a vase of silk flowers, framed photos of her friends and family, a carved marble award recognizing her accomplishments with the company, and a small solitary mahogany box that now seemed surprisingly out of place. She closed her fingers carefully around the simple beveled edge and removed it from its perch. Blowing accumulated dust from the lid, Olivia carried the box to her desk, cleared a space and slowly opened it.

Sure enough, her cherished bookmark with Mack's message accompanied another weathered piece of paper, both placed carefully in the box for safe keeping. Unfolding and smoothing them she wondered how long it had been since she last looked at them. A small shower of sand that had been trapped in the paper's folds landed on the surface of her desk. The first page was as clear today in its simple directive as it had been so many years ago when Mack handed it to her. The simplicity of that single word raised goose bumps on her arms.

The second sheet was much less formal and had been collected through contacts with the special people who shared those beached days with her. Her own message started the list:

SIMPLIFY FIRST

She laughed aloud and shook her head as she viewed the stacks piled on her desk. Continuing on, she read:

CONNECT DELIBERATELY
RETHINK YOUR WAY
MAKE WISE DECISIONS
CHOOSE TO SEE
CONTRIBUTE
BE PRESENT

Ringing loudly, the phone competed for her attention, and this time it won. "Hey Jay," Olivia said with no attempt to mask the elation in her voice. "I'm walking out the door." This familiar end-of-day script was one that both of them had grown comfortable with and could certainly repeat verbatim. "Uh huh, me too," she continued as she simultaneously turned off her computer. "Meet you there in twenty."

Appreciating again the real power of her time on the beach, Olivia looked around and felt as if she were seeing her office for the first time. Maybe she should have those messages framed. *Nah*, she decided, refolding and returning them to the box.

Picking up her briefcase and turning out the overhead light she took one last look at the dusty box sitting on the sandy surface of her desk. There was comfort in leaving it there to be rediscovered tomorrow with fresh eyes and renewed awe.

The sand on her desk shimmered and there was an almost flickering glow coming off of it. On other days she might have dismissed the vision as a result of being tired. But today she recognized the power, the magic, and the gift, of being beached.

Mack

Days counted off methodically, beached people came and went, sunrises and sunsets marked beginnings and endings. Like a fiery cauldron of liquid gold, Mack watched the sun begin its slippery descent from the day's blazing path across the sky. Losing strength and brilliance with every inch, it inevitably reached the lighthouse and blasted final gleaming rays against the enormous, glass turret. Mack stood firmly on the iron-grated walk that circled the lighthouse watching the day's activities, on the beach, and on the water, come to an end.

Focusing on the horizon, he never failed to marvel at the determined movement of the ships at this hour. Massive freighters driving forcefully, continuously, and dependably slowed their hustle while providing a stable backdrop for smaller enterprise, education, hospitality, and service ships to wrap up the day. Smaller vessels responding to last minute, impromptu missions shuttled in between the crawling steel gray, industrial giants. Sensing the close of day and the promise of evening quiet, seals, dolphins, and sea gulls broke the stillness with their last call for dinner and rush to find safety for the night.

The sun's rays lay across Mack's back sending comforting warmth to his bones. Looking down at his gloved hands resting on the sea-weathered railing, he inhaled the salt air. He quietly reflected on the importance of the evening tasks at the lighthouse, now completed, in anticipation of the approaching dark.

Through the open grate of the extended deck, Mack looked at the straight free-fall from the rock wall to the jagged and formidable rock outcropping below. He considered how tenuous his position might appear to others. Standing atop such an obvious risk, he nonetheless gave confidence to the aged and weather-beaten base holding him. His comfort lay in knowing the lighthouse as an old friend, having shared priceless care of each other year after year.

Waves crashed, lapping and retreating from the craggy shore below, performing an evening dance of competing tides. That which brought sustenance to shore life simultaneously eroded solid rock chunks and shell fragments returning them to the sea. A marvelous show unfolded beneath him.

An odd jangling noise diverted Mack's attention pulling his gaze toward the basin-shaped tide pool below. In the clear water a brown glass trespasser clinked against the rock-lined bowl. Bobbing gently in response to the rising and falling water, the corked bottle posed as an unwelcome intruder in this safe and orderly universe of the resident sea anemones, starfish, crabs, and guppies. If they could have, they certainly would have ejected it with rude determination and definitive urgency. "Don't fret, my friends," Mack muttered.

Descending to ground level he made his way to the water's edge. Slipping his gloves off and then reaching into the pool, he extracted the offending bottle. Holding it up to the waning light he noticed a curled paper inside. Stepping back onto the dry sand, he released the cork, and turned the bottle upside down. With a steady and experienced hand, Mack coaxed the paper from its glass protection, past the bottle's neck and into the evening light. Placing the cork back in the bottle, he tucked it into his jacket pocket. Carefully he unrolled the familiar stationery.

PERSEVERE

There, in his hands, was the formal note he regularly handed departing and previously beached friends. Happily, he remembered the variety of ways he distributed that farewell gift message to beached guests: tucked in a pocket, palmed unexpectedly in a handshake, or presented intentionally, with flourish and ceremony.

Recalling the reactions of those who discovered the solitary word penned on linen paper, Mack laughed as he mentally relived those moments watching that single powerful bullet hit its mark.

Regardless of each exclusive discussion, each special message, each fire ring conversation, each dream or goal, Mack knew individual success would ultimately lay in the value of implementing this last and critical action.

Persevere: never give up, never give in, and persist in all things good. Mack unrolled the paper completely and held the unfurled sheet gently, enjoying the paper's texture against his fingers.

There was his message, as clear as the day he delivered it—*persevere*. With a wave that began in his toes, warming him as methodically and visibly as the sun, Mack laughed at the simplicity and power of the response matching the size and intensity of his own, and read the new words

I AM.

Then, reading on, he saw in smaller, more personal script,

Thanks Mack

With a familiar, mixed sense of completion, pride, and anticipation, with the sunset at his back and a soft breeze upon his neck, Mack replaced the paper in the messenger bottle, pocketed it, pulled on his gloves, called to his playful canine friend, and began his evening walk up the beach.

"So, either you, or someone you know is *beached* . . . now what?"

Take a moment, build a bridge, find a way to apply what the book, the messages, the characters, and their stories mean to you or to someone in your life. BEACHED is more than a parable about dealing with challenges and change. It is an opportunity for you to recognize that we all are beached at one time or another and that while the majority of situations are temporary, we all need help to gain traction and successfully move forward in our personal and business lives.

For your consideration:

1. Of the six messages, which one is most relevant and applicable to your life now? Why?

2. Messages in this story are uniquely delivered. How do you respond to messages that come in unexpected ways?

3. Which of the six messages, seven including Olivia's, do you tend to share when someone you care about is beached? How might you deliver your message to them?

4. Mack is an advocate for those who are beached. Who is an advocate in your life? In whose lives are you an advocate?

5. If you were to meet Mack, what question or comment would you have for him? What impact might that interaction have on your life?

6. Recount a situation when you've been beached.
   What was the most powerful message you received?
   Who was your greatest advocate?
   What was the single most compelling lesson learned?

7. Were you sorry to see the book end?

Will you share your story about being beached?
Would you like to join a group talking about *Beached*?

You are invited to www.beachedstory.com to view the
website, share your story, engage in conversation,
and learn more about *Beached*.

Liz Beerman is available for group presentations or
workshops. She welcomes your inquiry at
lrbeerman@beachedstory.com.

Photograph by Tommy Collier,
Empire Mediaworks, Denver, CO

Liz Beerman obtained a Bachelor's degree in Psychology and a Master's in Education before engaging in high tech distribution and marketing, and then in worldwide business training.

As a mother of two sons, a partner of over thirty years, and a contributing member of her community, Liz has personally experienced the challenges and successes acquired when one is beached. She has had the good fortune to call both California and Colorado home and currently resides in a suburb of Denver, Colorado.

She is available for speaking engagements, workshops, and coaching on "Successfully moving forward when personal or business challenges leave an individual or business team beached."

Contact Liz at LRBeerman@BeachedStory.com

Susanne Leasure (front cover artist) and her true love and fellow artist Paul, since marrying in 2001, have lived and explored across the US. From Carpinteria and Los Osos, California, to windswept dunes and spectacular vistas of Montana de Oro State Park and the famous big Sur coastline, to North Carolina and now Texas.

Susanne creates images that capture the essence of an untainted Earth, the pristine beauty she hopes will remain forever. "Being an artist is not a profession; it is an intrinsic part of who I am. Art and soul are inseparable!"

http://www.lovefineart.com/susanne-leasure
LoveFineArt@gmail.com

Ken Ouellette (back cover photographer) resides in Colorado with a special place in his heart for the mountains of the West on which he has hiked, climbed, and photographed over the years.

Ken is ever exploring the sense of mood that is felt through his images. Working with the "magic of light" he is always searching for the exact moment when an image becomes a true artistic creation.

www.kenouellettephotography.com
kenouellettephotography@comcast.net

www.ingramcontent.com/pod-product-compliance
Lightning Source LLC
Chambersburg PA
CBHW020939090426
42736CB00010B/1199